Gospel of Su...

Søren Kierkegaard

Translated by

A. S. Aldworth and W. S. Ferrie

James Clarke & Co
Cambridge

First published 1955
Paperback edition 1982

ISBN 0 227 67860 5

© James Clarke & Co 1955

Published by
James Clarke & Co
7 All Saints' Passage
Cambridge
CB2 3LS
England

Printed in the United Kingdom by
Redwood Burn Limited, Trowbridge, Wiltshire,
and bound by Pegasus Bookbinding, Melksham, Wiltshire.

CONTENTS

		Page
I.	What is involved in the concept of following Christ; in particular, what joy is involved in it?	13
II.	How can the burden indeed be light, since suffering is heavy?	27
III.	The joy in the thought that the school of sufferings forms us for eternity.	47
IV.	The joy in the thought that before God a man is always accounted guilty.	65
V.	The joy in the thought that it is not the way that is narrow, but narrowness is the way.	93
VI.	The joy in the thought that even when time's suffering is heaviest eternity's blessedness still outweighs it.	112
VII.	The joy in the thought that in the midst of suffering, courage can wrest from the world its power, and can turn contempt to honour, disaster to triumph.	128

TRANSLATORS' INTRODUCTION

This is the third part of that trilogy which Kierkegaard published in 1847 as *Opbyggelige Taler i Forskellig Aand*. The first part consisted of what is sometimes called the "long" discourse, on the text, *Purify Your Hearts*, a "moral" analysis of doublemindedness. (It was translated by us and published in 1937, the first of Kierkegaard's works to be published in England.) The second part (also translated by us and published in 1940) was *Consider the Lilies*, an "æsthetic" contemplation on what it means to be a man. And now the seven discourses that follow in this volume are definitely "religious", with an ultimate appeal neither to the moral imperative nor to the æsthetic sense, but to faith. Thus is well illustrated the distinction Kierkegaard insisted on, the distinction of faith from ethics on the one hand and from æsthetics on the other.

The phrase "i forskellig aand" is capable of meaning not only "in a different vein", but "in different veins", or "in various modes". But we prefer to render it here "in a different vein" for a special reason. The volume of *Opbyggelige Taler* published by Kierkegaard in 1847 marked a departure from the series of Edifying Discourses that preceded it. The writer now sought to be not only edifying but definitely religious, and that in a Christian sense.

He had supposed that his work as an author was finished when he published, earlier in the same year, the *Concluding Unscientific Postscript*. But now it was to begin all over again, on a higher plane, as it were. The occasion for this new departure can be studied in Dr. Lowrie's *Kierkegaard*, and in Kierkegaard's own *Journals*, translated by Alexander Dru (Oxford University Press, 1938).

One element in the situation was the campaign of cheap ridicule launched against him by the journal *Korsaren*. This made him acutely aware of opposition and isolation. It also constituted a challenge, so that instead of retiring to a country parish, he resolved to remain in Copenhagen and contend for what he believed in. So he was made aware of tribulation as an inevitable part of following Christ.

The true preacher, it has been said, will preach out of his own experience, but he will not talk about himself. The pages that follow bear witness how far that is true of Kierkegaard. In one place, in the fourth discourse, he seems explicitly to endorse the popular opinion that the greatest human unhappiness is unhappy love. Of his own unhappy love, enough—perhaps too much!—has already been written. But besides that there are evidences here, particularly in the seventh discourse, that he found the scorn of his contemporaries a bitter draught to swallow. Nevertheless he would himself have been the last to wish his readers to find in what he wrote a mere self-disclosure. Not what distinguished him from others, but what he had in common with others—or rather let us say, what others may, if they will, find that they have in common with him—this constitutes the theme of these discourses. The theme is our sufferings. It is also the gospel that pertains to, and is appropriate to, our sufferings. It is in the realm of faith, and through this gospel that is the peculiar property of those who suffer, that sufferings are found to contain joys. We may say therefore that it is the purpose of this volume to disclose the meaning in the most meaningless element of life. Which might be held to be quite a good definition of the Christian faith.

In conclusion, we quote from the author's preface to Part I: "It is the individual whom with joy and gratitude I call my reader, the individual, willing to read slowly, to read repeatedly, and to read aloud—for himself to hear."

A. S. A.
W. S. F.

I

LUKE XIV. 27: *And whosoever doth not bear his cross, and come after me, cannot be my disciple.*

GUIDANCE enough indeed is offered us upon the way of life, and this is not surprising, since every leading astray claims to be guidance. But even if the ways of error be many, yet is the truth but one, but that One who is "the Way and the Life", the unique guidance which surely leads a man through life to Life. Thousands upon thousands bear a name to denote that they have chosen this guidance, that they belong to the Lord Jesus Christ, from whom they take the name of Christians, that they are his vassals, whether, for the rest, they be masters or servants, bond or free, men or women. *Christians* they call themselves, and they call themselves by other names as well which all denote a relation to this unique guidance. They call themselves *Believers*, which is to say that they are pilgrims, strangers and foreigners in the world. No pilgrim indeed is so surely recognised by the staff in his hand—many a one might carry a staff who is not upon a journey!—as calling oneself a believer is the accepted evidence of being a pilgrim. For to believe means precisely this, that what I am seeking is not here, and that is the very reason why I have faith in it. Faith means just that blessed unrest, deep and strong, which so urges the believer onward that he cannot settle at ease in this world, and anyone who was quite at ease would cease to be a believer. For a believer cannot sit still, as a man might sit with a pilgrim's staff in his hand; a believer journeys on. They call themselves *the Communion of Saints*, by which to denote what they are supposed to be and what they ought to be, what they hope to become some day, when faith shall be put aside and the pilgrim's staff laid down. They call themselves *Brethren of the Cross*, by which to denote that their way through the world is not as light as a dance, but heavy and toilsome, even though their faith be to them also the joy that overcomes the world. For as the ship, with sail set, lightly flies before the wind, yet ploughs a deep and heavy furrow in the sea, so too the Christian's way is easy, looking to the faith that overcomes the world, but heavy, looking to the toil and labour of the road-maker. They call themselves *Followers of Christ*, and it is on this name we now shall dwell, to consider:

WHAT IS INVOLVED IN THE CONCEPT OF FOLLOWING CHRIST; IN PARTICULAR, WHAT JOY IS INVOLVED IN IT.

When the bold warrior presses forward nothing daunted, and takes in his breast the arrows of the foe, thus protecting his young henchman who follows him, can we indeed say the youth is following him? When the loving wife, in what she holds the dearest in the world, in her husband, thinks she has the fine example she would like herself to attain in life, and so, womanlike—for woman was taken from man's side—walks by her husband's side, and finds support in him, can we indeed say this wife is following her husband? When the courageous teacher calmly takes his stand, surrounded by derision, pursued by envy, and all attacks are directed at him alone, and no one can even take aim at the disciple who is joined with him, can we indeed say that this disciple is following him? When the hen, seeing an enemy approach, spreads out her wings to provide a cover for the chickens behind her, can we indeed say that these chickens are following the hen? Nay, we cannot say so; the case must be altered. The bold warrior must withdraw, so that it may be seen now whether his henchman will truly follow him, follow him in actual danger, when all the shafts are aimed at *his* breast, or whether like a coward he will turn his back on danger, and lose his courage because he has lost his man of courage. As for the noble husband, he must step aside, must go away from her, alas, that now it may be seen whether the sorrowing widow lacking his support will follow him, or whether, because she is bereft of his support, she will let his example also go. The fearless teacher must hide himself, or must be hidden in a grave, that now it may appear whether his disciple will follow him, will stand his ground, surrounded by derision and pursued by envy, or whether he will depart from his position, in life, dishonourably, because his teacher honourably departed from it in his death.

To follow therefore means to go the way he went whom you are following; it means, that is to say, that he no longer is seen going. And thus was it necessary that Christ should go away, should die, before it could be shown whether his disciple would follow him. It is many, many hundreds of years since this took place, and yet in the same manner still it is forever taking place. For there is a time when Christ goes almost visibly by the child's side, when Christ goes on before the child, but then there is also a time when he is taken from the view of sensitive imagination, so that now the seriousness of decision may show whether the child, grown older, will follow him.

When a child is allowed to hold on to his mother's dress, can we say that then he is walking along with her, just as his mother walks? Nay, we may not say so. First must the child learn to walk alone and on his own, before he can go the way his mother goes, and go as she is going. And when the child is learning to walk alone, what must the mother do? She must make herself invisible. That her tenderness towards him is the same and remains unaltered, that indeed it probably grows greater, just at the time when the child is learning to walk alone, we know very well; the child, on the other hand, may not always understand it. But what is meant by the child having to learn to walk alone and to walk on his own, is, in a spiritual sense, the task set anyone who is to be somebody's follower—he must learn to walk alone and to walk on his own. Strange, is it not? Although it is almost as to something comical and always with a smile that we refer to the anxious efforts of the child to walk alone, yet language has no more forceful expression, and none more touching or more true, than this description of the deepest sorrow and suffering: to walk alone and to walk on one's own. That heaven's care for us is unchanged, and is indeed, were it possible, still more solicitous in this hour of danger, we know very well, but perhaps we cannot always understand it, when we are learning. So then to follow means to walk alone and to walk on one's own, the way the teacher went: to have nobody in sight with whom to take counsel, to be compelled to choose for oneself, to cry out in vain, as the child cries in vain, because the mother dare not seem to help; to despair in vain, because nobody is able to help, and heaven dare not appear to help. But to have invisible help, this is precisely learning to walk alone, for it is learning to transform one's mind to the likeness of the teacher's, though the teacher has passed from sight. To walk alone! Even so, for there is none, not any mortal man, who can choose for thee, nor in any final or decisive way give counsel in what belongs to the one matter of consequence, give counsel to decide in the matter of thy soul's welfare; and even if there were plenty willing to do so, it were without question but to thy hurt. Alone! For when thou hast chosen, thou shalt no doubt find companions of the way, but in the moment of decision, and whenever there is peril of life, then thou art alone. There is none who hears thy coaxing plea, nor heeds thy passionate complaining—yet is there help and willingness enough in heaven; but it is not seen, and to be helped by it is just to walk alone. Not from without this help doth come, to clasp thy hand, lending support as kindness helps the infirm, nor by compulsion comes to lead thee back, when thou hast gone astray. Nay, but only when thou dost yield completely, dost give up self-will, give thyself over with thy whole heart and soul, then in form unseen the help doth come; but just so hast thou walked upon thine own. We do not see the mighty urge that leads the bird on its long way; the urge flies not before and the bird behind it; it seems as if it were the bird that found the way: so we see not the teacher, but the follower only, who is like him, and it seems as if the follower were himself the way. For he is the true follower who goes along the same way, going alone.

This is what is implied in the concept: to follow anybody. But to *follow Christ* means, to take up the cross, or as in the text we have read, to bear the cross. To bear the cross means to deny oneself, as Christ makes plain, when he says: "If any man will come after me, let him deny himself, and take up his cross, and follow me" (Matt. xvi. 24). It was also this mind "which was in Christ Jesus, who thought it not robbery to be equal with God, but humbled himself . . . and became obedient unto death, even the death of the cross" (Phil. ii. 5f.). Such was the pattern, and such must the following be; even though it be a weary and a toilsome labour to deny oneself, a heavy cross to take up, a heavy cross to drag, yet is it, as the pattern requires, to be borne in an obedience unto death, so that the follower, though he may not die on the cross, still resembles his pattern in dying "with the cross on him".[1] One good deed, one high resolve, is not to deny oneself. That, alas, is what we may be taught in the world, because even that is so rarely seen that on the rare occasion we regard it wondering. But not so does Christianity teach us. Christ did not only say to the rich young man: "If thou wilt be perfect, sell all thou hast and give to the poor." To many this demand by itself might well appear excessive and odd; if the young man did this, perhaps he would not even be admired, but smiled at for an oddity, or pitied for a fool. But when Christ speaks he speaks otherwise; he says "Go thy way, sell that thou hast and give to the poor, and come, take up thy cross, and follow me" (Mark x. 21). And so to sell your goods and give to the poor is not to take up your cross, or at most it is the beginning, the good beginning, of going on to take up your cross and follow Christ. To give all to the poor is the first thing, it is, without unduly straining the words, *to take up the cross*; the next thing,

---

[1] Possibly a reference to Gal. vi. 17.

the long and weary sequel, is, *to bear one's cross*. Every day it must take place, not once and for all; and there must be nothing, nothing, that the follower is not willing to give up in self-denial. Whether it be something, as we say, of little account, wherein he is not willing to deny himself, or whether it be something great, does not make the least essential difference, for what is of little account is just what becomes of infinite account as it is the guilty occasion of a wrong relation to the self-denial demanded. Perhaps there was one who was willing to do what the rich young man did not do, and hoped that so he might have fulfilled the highest demand, who yet did not become a follower, because he remained standing— "turned round and looked back"[1] after his great achievement; or if he went on still did not become a follower, because in his opinion, when he had done such a great thing, what was less did not matter. Alas, whence comes it that the most difficult of all achievements should be to deny oneself in lesser things! May it not be because there is a certain refined self-love which also appears to be capable of self-denial in what is great? But the less the demand, the more paltry, so much the more does it offend this self-love, because for such a duty it is quite deprived of its own and other people's extravagant praise; and that is why self-denial is all the humbler. Whence comes it that the most difficult achievement is for a man to deny himself when he lives alone and, as it were, in an obscure corner! May it not be, I wonder, because a certain refined self-love also appears to be capable of self-denial—when there are many admirers looking on! But just as it makes no essential difference, what are the different interests in which each individual, according to his circumstances, exercises self-denial, so that a beggar can exercise the same absolutely real self-denial as a king: so does it make no essential difference what are the different interests in which a man refrains from self-denial; for self-denial is nothing else but the deep inward spirit of denying oneself.

[1] Reference to Luke ix. 62?

And this is a heavy, burdensome task. For no doubt self-denial consists in throwing off burdens, and so might seem a light enough task; but it is indeed a heavy one, to have to throw off just those burdens, which self-love would so dearly like to bear, aye, so dearly, that it is only with the greatest difficulty that self-love can come to understand that they are burdens.

To follow Christ means therefore to deny oneself, and so it means *to go by the same way* as Christ went, in the humble form of a servant, in want and scorn and mockery, not loving the world, and not beloved by it. And so it means *to walk alone*, for one who in self-denial forsakes the world and all that is of the world renounces everything that might allure and might distract him,[1] so that he does not go to his field, nor strike a bargain, nor take to himself a wife. One who, if need be, does not indeed love father and mother, sister and brother,[2] less than before, but loves Christ so much more that he can be said to hate those others, he walks alone indeed, alone in the whole world. It is true that in the multifarious cross-currents of the activities of the world it appears difficult, indeed impossible, to live like this, impossible even to judge whether anybody actually does live like this; but let us not forget that it is eternity that shall judge how the problem was solved, and that the seriousness of eternity shall command a shamefaced silence about all that is of the world, about all that was forever talked of in the world. For in eternity thou shalt not be asked how great are the possessions thou art leaving behind thee—this question is for those who *survive* thee to ask!—or how many battles thou hast won, how wise thou wast, how powerful thine influence—this will be thy *fame in time to come*! Nay, eternity shall not ask about *what of the world remains behind thee* in the world. But it shall ask what treasure thou hast stored up in heaven; how often thou hast overcome thine own soul, what self-mastery thou hast achieved, or whether thou hast been in bondage; how often thou hast in self-denial

---

[1] Luke xiv. 26.   [2] Luke xiv. 17-20.

been thine own master, or if thou hast never been so; how often thou hast in self-denial been willing to make an offering to a good cause, or if thou hast never been so willing; how often thou hast in self-denial forgiven thine enemy, whether seven times or seventy times seven; how often thou hast in self-denial borne patiently humiliations; and what thou hast suffered, not for thine own sake, not for the sake of thy selfish purposes, but what thou hast in self-denial suffered for the sake of God.

And he who shall judge thee, the judge from whose judgment thou canst not appeal to any higher, he was not the captain of a host, conquering kingdoms and lands, with whom to speak of thy worldly feats, but his kingdom was one not of this world; he was not one robed in purple, with whom to hope to be in distinguished company, for he bore the purple only as the butt of mockery; he was not powerful through his influence, so that he might wish to be initiated into thy worldly schemes, for he was so despised that the ruler dared to visit him only under cover of the night. Oh, but it were very comforting to meet together with those who are like-minded; when one is cowardly, not to be indicted before a court of warriors, when one is self-loving and worldly not to be called in judgment by self-denial. And this judge not only knows what self-denial is, not only knows how to judge so that no offence can be concealed, nay, but to be in his presence is to be judged, his presence that makes everything keep silence and turn pale which, being of the world, in the world looked well, was heard and seen with admiration; his presence is the judgment, for he *was* self-denial. He, who was the equal of God, took upon himself the humble form of a servant; he, who could exercise command over legions of angels, yea, over the world, that it should exist or be destroyed, went about defenceless; he, who had all power, gave up all power, and could do nothing even for his dear disciples but offer them the same terms of lowliness and contempt; he, who was Lord of creation, made Nature herself be dumb, for it was only when he had given up the ghost that the veil was rent and the graves were opened, and the forces of Nature betrayed who he was: if this is not self-denial, then what is self-denial!

This is what was implied in the concept of following Christ; but now let us consider *the joy that is in it.*
My hearer! If thou wouldst suppose a youth standing at life's beginning, where the many ways open out before him, and asking himself which course he would wish to pursue: does he not make close enquiry whither each one leads, or, what is the same thing, try to find out who has gone that way before? Then we name to him the famous, the worthy, the glorious names of those whose memory is preserved among men. To begin with, we recite so many names, that the choice may have some relation to the youth's possibilities, and so that there may be no stint of the wealth of alternatives offered; but he himself, urged by the craving in his soul, now makes a narrower choice, and finally there remains to him one only name, the one that in his eyes and in his heart is the finest of them all. Then his heart thrills when with enthusiasm he names this name, for him the only one, and says: By this way will I go, for by this way went he!
But we shall not now divide attention or waste time naming such names; for there is in the end but one name in heaven and upon earth, one only name, and hence but one way to choose—if a man is to choose seriously and to choose aright! Since a man has to choose, there must be more ways than one; but also there must be only one way to be chosen, if the seriousness of eternity is to be in the choice. A choice of which it can be said that one might just as well choose the one way as the other does not have the seriousness of eternity; there must be in the choosing absolutely all to win and all to lose, if the choice is to have the seriousness of eternity, even though, as we have said, there must be a possibility of choosing between alternatives, that the choice may really be a choice.
There is but one name in heaven and on earth, but one

way, and but one pattern. He who chooses to follow Christ, chooses that name which is above every name,[1] that pattern which is highly exalted above all heavens, which yet is so truly human that it can be a pattern for a human being, and so shall be named in heaven and on earth, in both places as the highest. For there are patterns whose name is named only on the earth, but the highest, the only name, must have this very character of uniqueness, from which again it is to be recognised as the only one: that it is named both in heaven and on earth. This name is the name of our Lord, Jesus Christ. But surely this is something joyous, that we should dare to choose to go the same way as he went! Alas! in the confused and confusing talk of the world, the simple and the serious sounds sometimes almost like a jest. That man who doubtless exercises the greatest power ever exercised in the world calls himself proudly the follower of Peter. But to be a follower of Christ! Truly that does not tempt a man to be proud; it is granted equally to the mightiest and the humblest, the wisest and the simplest; which is again just what is blessed about it. And is it so very glorious a thing to be that Highness which no other can become; is it not rather dreary! Is it so glorious a thing to dine off silver when others go hungry, to dwell in palaces when so many have no shelter, to be the great scholar no simple man can be, to have a name in a sense in which thousands upon thousands are excluded: is that so glorious! And if this—this envious distinction—were the highest our life on earth could offer, would it not offer an inhuman and intolerable fate to the fortunate man! But how different, on the contrary, when the only joy is to follow Christ! Greater joy there cannot be than this—to be able to become what is highest; and this supreme joy cannot be made more full of courage, more blessed, more confident than it is already, with its joyful thought, given by *heaven's loving kindness*: that it is in the power of every man.

So the man who chose to follow Christ goes forward on the way. And when he must also learn to know the world and

[1] Phil. ii. 9.

what is in the world, the world's strength and his own weakness, when the struggle with flesh and blood distresses him, when the going is heavy, and there are many foes and no friends, then the agony of it may well wring from him the moan: I walk alone.

Listen to me. If a child learning to walk came crying, and said to his mother: I am walking alone, would she not answer: Isn't that splendid, child! And so also with the following of Christ. On this way, it is not only true to say, as is said elsewhere, that when need is greatest help is nearest, nay, but here, on this way, the greater the suffering the nearer to perfection. Is there any other way known where this is true? On every other way it is the reverse that is true: if sufferings come, the weight of them outweighs all else. So much so, that it may even indicate the wrong way has been chosen. But on that way where a man follows Christ, the height of suffering is the height of glory. Even as the pilgrim moans, in his heart he reckons himself to be in bliss.

See how a man setting out on any other way must first make himself familiar with the uncertainties of it: it may go well, and without any difficulties, but there may also be so many obstacles heaped up that he can make no progress. In following Christ on the way of self-denial, there is, on the contrary, the perfection of assurance; for on this way the "marks" of suffering are the joyous signs that the right way is being followed. But what joy can be greater than to dare to choose the best way, the way to the highest! And again, what joy so great as this, except the joy of the infinite security of the way!

Yet there remains one last blessed joy in the concept of following Christ. For in truth he, who was revealed, does not go with his follower, neither does he go visibly in front of him, but he has gone *before*, and this is his follower's joyful hope: that he shall follow where he has gone. It is one thing to follow him on the way of self-denial, and this itself were joyous; it is another thing to follow him into eternal bliss. When death has divided two who were lovers, and then the survivor dies, we say: She has followed him now—he had gone before. So Christ went before, and not only so, for he went to *prepare a place for his follower*.[1]

When it is a human forerunner of whom we are speaking, then it may be true to say that by going on before he has made the way easier for one who comes after; and when the way about which we are speaking refers to the earthly, the temporal, the imperfect, then it may even happen that the way has been made quite easy for the follower. This is not true with reference to the Christian or with reference to the perfect way of self-denial; it is essentially the same hard way for every follower. But then it is in quite another sense that we say of Christ, he went before: he did not by going before prepare the way for his follower, but he went before to prepare for his follower a place in heaven. A human forerunner at times may justly say: Now it is easy enough to come on behind, when the road has been laid down and made ready and the gate is wide. Christ, on the other hand, must say: Behold, all is ready in heaven—if thou art ready to enter in by the strait gate, and to go forward on the narrow way, of self-denial.

In the preoccupations of the world it may seem very doubtful about this place in the beyond; but the man who in self-denial has renounced the world and himself must have assured himself in doing so that such a place exists. Somewhere indeed must that man be who does exist, and somewhere have his habitation; but in the world he has renounced he can have no place: hence there must be some other place, there must be, if he is even to be able to make the renunciation. Oh, is this not quite simply understood by anybody who has really denied himself and the world! And to stake one's life on the question whether one be really confident that there is such a place in the beyond, whether one actually is assured of eternal life, is simple too. The Apostle Paul says (1 Cor. xv. 19): "If in this life only we have hope in Christ, then are we of all men most miserable." And it is so indeed, because any man who for

[1] John xiv. 2.

Christ's sake renounces all the good things of the world and endures all its evils, if there be no blessedness in the beyond, is deceived, horribly deceived. If there be no blessedness in the beyond!—to me it seems that it would have to be, if only from sympathy with such a man. So that if a man does not set his mind on earthly things and on good times, does not yearn for worldly gain, nor even grasp it when it is offered, if he chooses toil and strain, and, as well may be, ungrateful labour, because he has chosen the better part, if when he must do without earth's reward, he has not even the consolation of knowing that he did all he could to earn it: then is he a fool in the eyes of the world, he is the miserable man of the world. Were there no blessedness in the beyond, then were he of all men most miserable, and it were just his self-denial that had made him so—him, who had not even striven to win earth's prize, but had of his free will renounced it. If, on the other hand, there is a blessedness beyond, then he, the miserable, is yet the richest of all men. For it is one thing to be the most miserable in the world, when the world is considered to be above all; it is another thing to be the most miserable in the world when blessedness is, or is to be, the highest. The proof that this blessedness exists is very finely stated by Paul; for there cannot be the slightest doubt that without it he had been of all men most miserable. But if a man strives to make himself secure in the world, tries to get himself the world's gain, then his assertion that there is a blessedness beyond is not quite convincing; it will scarcely convince others, it has scarcely convinced himself. But let none sit in judgment on this, or each upon his own case only, for the very readiness to judge another in this matter is an attempt to secure one's own position in the world; else one would realise that both judgment and blessedness belong to another world.

Ah, in the course of time it has often happened, and still it keeps on happening again and again, that someone goes before for whom another yearns and whom he fain would follow: but never has anyone, any loved one, any teacher, any friend, gone on before—to prepare a place for him who follows! As Christ's is the only name in heaven and on earth, so too Christ is the only forerunner who has thus gone before. There is between heaven and earth only one way: to follow Christ; both in time and in eternity there is but one choice, one only: to choose this way; on earth there is but one hope of eternity, to follow Christ to heaven. In life there is one blessed joy: to follow Christ; and in death there is one final blessed joy: to follow Christ into Life!

II

MATTHEW XI. 30: *My yoke is good,*[1] *and my burden is light.*

OF the Pharisees it is said: "They bind heavy burdens and grievous to be borne and lay them on men's shoulders; but they themselves will not move them with one of their fingers" (Matt. xxiii. 4). And this way of behaving, unhappily, is found quite frequently repeated in the world. It is repeated in such a relation as might seem to justify distinguishing between one who bears the burden and one who is exempted. But in truth there is no justification for the distinction, for one must bear the ruler's, and another the subject's burden, one the teacher's and another the pupil's burden, and so forth, none being exempted, not even the independent person, who must bear a burden of responsibility, as the dependent person bears that of obligation. This same pharisaic way of behaving is found also in that relation of which we can say that two must pull together in the same yoke, so that one of them is disposed merely to bind the burdens and lay them on the other, the husband demanding everything of the wife, or the wife of her husband; or in the relation of friendship, of partnership, where there is no equality, but one demands everything of his friend, of his fellow-worker, in order that he himself may be free. Indeed, we may see not only this, but behaviour still more pitiful, when one is so ungrateful or so lacking in appreciation or so capricious as to add to the weight of the burden an extra weight, making the selfish demand that the other shall bear the burden, and then making it hard for him to bear.

This is not just a cynical and ill-humoured way of describing the world as it is in these days of ours. On the contrary; it is

---

[1] Greek, χρηστός, rendered in Danish by *gavnlig*, i.e. beneficial, or, in an archaic sense, "easy".

a hoary reflection, found apt to the most diverse times by the greatest diversity of people. So that mankind, though akin to the divine, is also, somehow or other, depraved. This is most easily seen when we consider man's Exemplar. For if man were not akin to God, there could not be for him any such Exemplar, yet on the other hand it is precisely when we contemplate the Exemplar that the depravity is seen to be more deeply dyed, and when we behold the purity of the Exemplar the darkness of the shadow of depravity is the blacker. This Examplar is the Lord Jesus Christ. He "came not to be ministered unto", not to lay burdens on others; he bore their burdens, that heavy burden which each and every man would fain refuse, the burden of sin, that heavy burden which not mankind itself could bear, the sin of the race. And it was made hard for him to bear it; he was despised and rejected, persecuted, mocked at, yea, he was by sinners delivered up unto death, he was, and he is, regarded by sinners as an enemy—because he is "the friend of sinners!" Yet did he bear the burden that the race had laid upon him, or that he had taken upon himself, and not only so, but the whole of his life and every moment of it was given up to the bearing of others' burdens. For we hear him say these words: "Come unto me all ye that labour and are heavy laden" (Matt. xi. 28); but never do we hear that he said: Nay, I have no time to-day; I am not in the mood to-day, for I have been invited to a feast; or: I have no inclination to-day, for I have had some anxiety myself; or: To-day I have lost patience with mankind, having been so often deceived. Never were any such words heard on his lips; else had there been, what Scripture denies, and what makes faith shudder, guile in his mouth,[1] for in his heart he would not have meant it! There was nobody's suffering so dreadful that he wished to be ignorant of it lest it should disturb his joy or increase his sorrow; for his sole joy was to find rest for the soul of the sufferer, and it was his greatest grief when the sufferer would not allow himself

---

[1] cf. 1 Pet. ii. 22.

to be helped. Wherever you might meet him, seeking solitude in a place apart, or frequenting temple or market-place in order to teach, he was willing immediately, and did not make the excuse that he wanted to be alone, nor make the excuse that he was busy. When those who were in one sense his nearest would abuse their kinship and demand his time, then he did not acknowledge them, but if there was a sufferer there, him he acknowledged. He came, when a ruler sent for him, and when, on the way, a woman touched the hem of his garment, he was not heard to say: Nay, stay me not! but he stayed. And when the disciples would hold back the crowd, he administered a rebuke.

Ah, if that were wisdom which we are all too prone to understand as wisdom, that every man's nearest neighbour is himself, then would the life of Christ be foolishness, for his life was sacrifice, so much so that he seemed to be nearest to everybody else and furthest from himself. But if he be the absolute, eternal Exemplar: then let us learn of him, as he himself bids us do (Matt. xi. 29): "Take my yoke, and learn of me"—let us learn of him to bear the burdens, both our own and others'.

Easy indeed were it, like a Pharisee, to lay the burden upon others, but hard to bear it oneself. Easy to promise in a moment of exaltation to bear the burden, but hard to bear it. Who knows this better than the sufferer, who is a sufferer just because he has his burdens to bear? And if anybody wants to hear sighing and moaning and crying, he may hear it in plenty from those who suffer. But there also it is true to say that it were easy enough to whine and moan and pity oneself, even over trivialities; this is something the sufferer does not need to learn, for it is pain that first teaches it, and pain is ready with a cry. But to endure with tight lips, or perhaps even find joy in the bitterness of suffering—and not find it only in the hope that the suffering will come to an end in time—but to find it in suffering, as when we say that sorrow is mixed with joy; this is something worth the learning.

But this is just the lesson that is contained in the sacred words we read: My yoke is good and my burden is light. And as it is said, so it is; though it may be found difficult for the sufferer to understand, as if this mild saying were a hard saying, because hard for the sufferer to grasp, so that he cries out in amazement:

BUT HOW CAN THE BURDEN BE LIGHT, SINCE THE SUFFERING IS HEAVY?

So now let us, not with that wonder of unbelief which in the exclamation would disguise denial, but with the wonder of faith, which is its own best evidence, and which is incredulous only in the praise of God, and then again is lost in happy wonder, let us with this wonder of faith consider the question. For it was by no means Christ's intention to lead men out of the world to realms of Paradise where was neither want nor misery, or as by a magician's wand to transform our life on earth into worldly joy and happiness. This was only a misconception of the Jews, superficial and frivolous. But he would teach, what he demonstrated by his example, how the burden is light even when the suffering is heavy. And so in one sense the burden remains the same, for the burden is just the suffering, the heavy suffering, and yet this burden has become light. Because Christianity has come into the world, man's lot has not thereby become another earthly lot than it was before. A Christian may have to suffer exactly as he suffered before, but yet for a Christian the heavy burden has become light. This, first, we shall ponder; and afterwards more especially consider what is the light burden the Christian in particular must bear.

When we talk about bearing burdens in the language of every day, we distinguish between a light burden and a heavy one; we say it is easy to bear the light burden, hard to bear the heavy one. But we are not speaking of this now; we speak of the far more solemn theme, that one and the same burden should be heavy and yet light; we speak of a miracle and a wonder—for is it any greater wonder to turn water into wine, than that a heavy burden should continue to be heavy and yet be light? And yet there are occasions when we do speak like this also. When a man, for instance, is at the point of sinking under the heavy burden he bears, but that burden is his dearest possession, then he says that it is a light burden. Such things are seen in the world. We look with horror on the miser who drags himself along under the killing weight of his treasure, yet counts this heavy burden light, because his treasure is his all. We contemplate in silent exaltation of spirit a man bearing what in a good sense is for him the most precious thing in the world, finding it truly heavy, and yet light. When one who loves is in distress in the sea, and at the point of drowning because of the weight of her whom he loves and whom he wants to save, then his burden is certainly heavy, and yet —yes, ask him!—yet so unspeakably light. Though there be two of them in danger of life, and the other pull him down, yet has he but one desire, to save his life; and so he is speaking as if the burden did not even exist, calling her his life, and he would save his life. How does this change come about? Is it not perhaps through a thought, an idea, that intervenes? The burden is heavy, he says. But now the thought or the idea interposes, and he says: Nay, ah nay, but how light it is! Is he then insincere because he speaks thus? Not at all; when he speaks truly thus, then he truly loves. And so it is by the power of the thought, of the idea, of love, that the change is brought about.

"*My yoke is good*"—anybody who may be described as a lucky fellow, or, probably more accurately, as a light-minded fellow, can easily enough stick his head in the air and hold it up. But anybody who goes bowed under the heavy yoke of suffering may be one who has never known how to do anything but sink under the weight, and so he goes bowed with bent head, and so is struck dumb without a word, without a thought, in his defeat. Without a thought, yes, for that is just what is wrong with him, that he has not a single thought to help him even to raise the burden to a higher plane. A thought is needed; if it is always needed, it is needed especially here, to mark man's superiority over the brute. Hence the fine uplifting words of a noble mind,[1] when, speaking of the earthly struggle, he asks for one thing only: Give me a great thought! And so there may be many splendid and precious thoughts, which, even if they could not make the yoke light yet could help to raise the burden; there might be the thought of better times one has had, or of the better times one hopes for, the thought of somebody one loves or of somebody one admires, the thought of what one owes to somebody else, or the thought of what one owes to oneself. Above all, however, there is one thought, and only one, capable of turning the balance, one thought which has the power of transforming by faith the heavy burden into a burden that is light, and this thought is that it is good, that the heavy burden is good for one.[2]

But that the heavy suffering is good is something that must be *believed*, because it cannot be seen. Perhaps we can see afterwards that it *has been* good, but at the time of suffering we can neither see it, nor, even though ever so many people with the best of motives keep on repeating it, can we hear it spoken; it must be believed. It is the thought of faith we need, and the earnest, confident, frequent expressing of this thought to ourselves. For if it be true that the word is the binding power, so that with a word one binds oneself for ever, then it is true also that the word is the loosening power, to loosen the yoke of bondage, so that the believer goes freely under the yoke, and also to loosen the tongue, so that he is no longer dumb, and his voice returns to worship. It must be believed. It is not difficult to see the joy when one beholds joy unmixed around one—this very statement is an almost absurd demonstration how easy it is. But when one looks on unmixed misery all around, then by faith to see the joy: yea, this is meet and

[1] Herder, *Zur Philosophie*, XVII.   [2] See footnote, p. 27.

proper. It is meet and proper so to speak of faith, for faith is always with reference to what is not seen, whether the *invisible* or the *improbable*; and it is meet and proper that a man have faith.

It is said of faith that it can move mountains. Even the heaviest suffering, however, cannot be heavier than a mountain, for the strongest way of expressing it is to say: Suffering weighs on a man like a mountain. But if a sufferer really believes that the suffering is good for him—why then, he moves mountains. And so we cannot doubt that there are those who in every step they take, are moving a mountain, who, every day they live, are moving a mountain. To move the mountain one must go beneath it, and thus, ah thus, does the sufferer submit to his heavy burden. This is what is hard. But the power of faith to endure under suffering, the belief that it is for his good, lifts the mountain up and moves it. A sufferer may listen to the kind and sympathetic and encouraging words of another, and perhaps be touched and moved when the other says: It is for thy good, but that does not enable him to move the mountain. A prisoner may listen with tears to the voice of his beloved without, but that does not set him free, sometimes it only makes captivity the harder. The sufferer may listen to these voices, but if he does not hear the same voice in his heart, then he cannot move the mountain. In his distress he may even refuse to listen to these voices; still less does this help him to move the mountain. If, however, he can believe that it is for his good, then he moves the mountain. For is it not true to say that this great mountain stands in his way, and he may if he likes go by another way or have the mountain taken out of his way, but if it is for his good, then his way is made for him. That is his way on which the mountain stands. The good that is in it gives the mountain, if I may put it so, its notice to quit. It was a good pagan who said: Give me a standing-point outside the world, and I will move the world.[1] Our prince of writers said: Grant me

[1] Archimedes.

a great thought. Ah, but the former is impossible, and the other does not altogether help us. One thing alone can help, though it cannot be given us by another: Have faith and thou shalt move mountains.

Have faith that the yoke is good for thee. This good yoke is Christ's yoke. But what then is signified by the yoke? There is no end to the variety of its significance, but only that yoke is Christ's yoke of which a sufferer believes that it is good for him. For it is not true that a Christian is exempt from the common lot of human suffering in the world. Nay, verily, yet he who so bears suffering as to believe his yoke is good for him, he bears Christ's yoke. Humanly speaking, no new suffering has been added, nor, on the other hand, has any old suffering been taken away; to that extent, all is as before. Yet it has now been granted, that great thought, and it has now been found, that standing-point outside the world—faith!

It is not an invention of worldly-wisdom, not its trivial, chattering concern with this that is good or that that is good; nay, it is quiet Faith, believing in goodness. With the help of worldly-wisdom one may crawl through the world, and contrive to avoid many troubles, talking oneself out of some, and excusing oneself from some, but all this is no more Faith than it is—to move mountains!

And so when faith holds on to the good that is in it, and moves the mountain, then such is the joy of faith that the yoke is actually light. In exact proportion as it is conceived to be heavy, when faith is nevertheless able to move it, just so light has it become. When anybody lifts a feather, he says: It is light, but when anybody goes up to a great load, looks at it, and despairs for his own strength, and yet attempts to lift it, and lo, the attempt succeeds: then he is so glad, that in the joy and amazement of the change he cries: It is light! Has the man become a fool then? Has he forgotten then that he despaired for his own strength? Has he then taken in vain the help of heaven? Not at all; it is just in the blessed amazement of faith that he speaks. If a maid, true to her woman's nature, has but one desire, and that, alas, kept secret in hopelessness, then she may say: It cannot be! Possibly this means that she has made herself indifferent, and would retire to her couch, to escape in sleep from her desire, in sleep to find forgetfulness; possibly it means that she will no longer cherish a hopeless desire. But if, on the other hand, true to her woman's nature, she brings all her soul to concentrate on the hope of her desire, and so achieves it, then too, on the very day of her rejoicing, she exclaims: It cannot be! Then, too, she acknowledges the truth with the most joyful greeting, with blessed amazement: It cannot be! Then, too, a long time must pass before she can persuade her heart to say: It is real! because every day it becomes to her as something beyond words more precious to greet the truth with the exclamation: It cannot be! Is she a fool then, trifling with facts? Is she then a graceless creature who does not know how to set a value on the fact? Not at all, she knows its worth, for this *is* to know its worth—to begin each day of realisation with the same wonder as before; being humble she believes humbly. Hers is the wonder of faith, and that she should continue to wonder is her faith in the Power that made the impossible possible. Consider! The foolish virgins represent a foolish expectation; but let us change the parable a little. Take the five wise ones who kept the lamp of expectation burning and went in with the bridegroom—had they said, as soon as the door was shut, Now all is settled and secure, might not their lamps also, I wonder, have been said in another sense to be out! But faith, it keeps the lamp alight; in waiting and in expectation keeps the lamp alight to the end; and if fulfilment comes, still keeps the lamp alight, in not forgetting that it was impossible. But he, on the other hand, who was impatient and found his yoke only heavy, while it *was* heavy; whenever the yoke is made light for him, still true to character will pervert the truth. For he will maintain the cheap deception, that what once he could not understand he now understands quite easily.

Nevertheless, this fulfilment of expectation must be waited

for. But we do not need to wait for the good that is in suffering; if only we do not demand the evidence of it (which is where we fail), if we are willing to believe, then it has come to pass. And therefore is the faith that heavy suffering is for our good more perfect far than the expectation of a happy ending. For the happy ending may not come about, but a believer believes the suffering is for his good, hence good cannot fail to come about—since it already is! A believer as a mortal man, knows how heavy suffering is; but with a faith that wonders that it should be for his good he says in spirit: It is light! As a man he says this is impossible, but he says it too with the wonder of faith that what as a man he cannot understand should yet be good for him. When worldly wisdom is capable of realising goodness, Faith is not capable of seeing God; but when worldly wisdom cannot see a hand's-breadth before it in the dark night of suffering, Faith can see God. For Faith sees best in the dark. When worldly-wisdom comforts a sufferer, this is how it goes about it. It says: Of course it will be quite all right and all very good in a little. And then takes the opportunity to depart. Just as when a doctor on his visit to a patient says: In a little while—and then departs, so that the patient never can get hold of the doctor to keep the cheat to his word, for the doctor has stolen away. But when Faith comforts a sufferer it plants itself beside him, and says: Thy suffering is for thy good; only believe that so it is. This thou canst by faith grasp here and now. And so I am going to stay with thee, that if I speak falsely thou mayst vent thine anger on me. For I need no time to pass, as if I were a casual passer-by. I need no time for passing like a cheat. Nay, it is for thy good. Let thy suffering increase, it is for thy good. This good exists, even as I exist—I, Faith! Such is the good that is known to Faith, and this good persists, even when Faith is tried, and when it seems Faith finds no favour with God, but only provokes him to try it more and more, the more this Faith abounds, so that to the believer in his despair it seems as if he might some day regret his faith—as if indeed that were the happy man who goes through life carefree, and never has anything at all to do with God, but saunters along the broad highway, or seeks the much-praised middle course, but never struggles onward, under the yoke, by the narrow way of faith. Nevertheless, whoever he be who lives that way, and whatever else he be, he is no Christian. Because to the Christian the yoke is for his good: this he believes.

One bears a yoke of iron, another a yoke of wood, a third a golden yoke, a fourth the heavy yoke, but only the Christian bears—the yoke that is good!

"*My burden is light.*" For what else is meekness but bearing the heavy burden lightly, just as it is impatience and fretfulness to bear the light burden heavily.

Language supplies us with a splendid word, ready to adapt itself in many connections, but never so eagerly as in connection with what is good. It is the word *Courage*.[1] Wherever goodness is, there courage too is found; whatever fate befall the good, courage is still forever on the side of goodness; the good is always courageous, only the evil is cowardly and afraid, and the devil always trembles.[2] This bold word, then, never turning from danger but always facing it, is in itself a proud word; yet how adaptable it is, when we find it sweetly amenable towards every kind of goodness! So is this bold word intolerant of all evil but consistently in harmony with all kinds of goodness.

There is Courage, bravely defying danger. There is the Generous Spirit, rising proudly superior to injuries. There is Long-suffering, which patiently endures. But the Spirit of Meekness, bearing what is heavy—lightly!—is quite the most wonderful conjugation of the word.[3] For it is nothing wonderful, with the strength of iron to take firm hold of the heaviest loads, but it is truly wonderful when one can with the strength

---

[1] In Danish, *Mod*.   [2] Jas. ii. 19.

[3] The point here cannot be brought out in English. In the original the words are ho*imod*, taal*mod*, and sagte *Mod*.

of iron take a gentle hold of the weakest, or lightly grasp what is heavy.

Yet it is to meekness that Christ urges his followers: Learn of me, for I am meek and lowly of heart. He himself was meek. He did indeed bear a burden, heavy far beyond human power —yea, beyond the power of the race to bear—and he bore it lightly. But when one bearing himself this heaviest of all burdens has time and readiness and sympathy and self-sacrifice to be always concerned for others, to help others, to heal the sick, to visit the wretched, to save the desperate, is he not bearing the burden lightly then? He bore the heaviest grief, grief for the fallen race, and yet so lightly did he bear it that he quenched no smoking flax, and broke no bruised reed.

As the Exemplar was, so ought also the follower to be. When anyone bears a heavy burden, but seeks for that reason the help of others, to lay some part of it on them, or when anyone bears a heavy burden, but for that reason has quite enough to think about in the mere bearing of his burden, then he is bearing his burden indeed, in part or altogether, but he is not bearing it lightly. When anyone must gather all his energies, and has not a single thought, nor a single moment, to spare for other people, and when thus he is bearing his burden to the limit of his power, he is indeed bearing it, but he is not bearing it lightly; he may be bearing it in a patient spirit, but he is not bearing it in a spirit of meekness. For Courage is strident, Generosity is proud, Patience is dumb, but Meekness bears the burden lightly. Courage we can see, and Generosity, and Patience is evident in the effort made, but Meekness renders itself invisible, seeming so easy though it is so hard. That there is Courage in it is seen in the eye, that there is Generosity is seen in the deportment and the expression, that there is Patience is seen from lips that are tight, but Meekness none may see.

What then is the meek spirit's light burden? Verily, it is the heavy burden when it is borne lightly. But what is the meek spirit's heavy burden? Verily, it can be infinitely various, but it is not this variety that counts in the weighing, but rather the meekness. The light burden of impatience can also be infinitely various, but it is not this variety that counts in the weighing, but rather the impatience, that makes it heavy— Impatience, which is not akin to Courage, or only belongs to the family as a degenerate member thereof.[1] But it is a veritable fact that, through meekness, in a divine sense the heavy burden becomes veritably light; just as it is an unhappy truth that through impatience the light burden becomes veritably heavy. What is good for us is the light yoke, and meekness is the light burden. There can never to all eternity be any doubt that that which is good for us is a light burden to bear, and therefore doubt seeks to draw attention elsewhere; it can quite well understand that whatever is good for us is light, but it will not believe that heavy suffering is that goodness. Meekness is a light burden, of that there can never to all eternity be any doubt; therefore doubt would draw attention elsewhere; it can understand quite well that meekness is light, but it will not understand that what is heavy should become a light burden through meekness, that the burden should become veritably light, which yet in fact it does.

And so when anyone who knows not to-day what life tomorrow may bring him, when he, as the Gospel bids him (for Christ came not into the world to banish care by giving prosperity), when he refuses to be anxious about the morrow, then is he bearing the burden lightly. While indeed there are not many who can be said to have enough to last their lifetime, on the other hand it may all too easily appear to any anxious one, whose vision is blurred by gazing on too remote a prospect, as if the cares of the world might go on for a yet longer period than his whole life. When thus it is, he is bearing the heavy burden heavily. But if he resolve patiently to bear the burden as long as it shall be required of him, he still is not bearing the burden lightly. The subtlest and strongest enemy is time, especially when it gathers itself to the attack and is known as

---

[1] Impatience, *utaalmodighed*; courage, *mod*.

time-to-come, for then it is like a mist which cannot be seen close to, but the more we contemplate it from a distance the more terrible it seems to be. When patience gazing tries to bear what-is-to-come, then it is seen how great a weight it is; but the meek spirit is not anxious, not even about the morrow. Meekness is quick to withdraw its gaze within itself and so it does not see the infinite time-to-come. It calls the time-to-come to-morrow. It is true that to-morrow is also time-to-come, but time-to-come seen as near as may be; so mildly does meekness behave, so warily does it deal with the time-to-come. Quite close to us, however, we cannot see the mist which when the eye is uncontrolled appears so terrible, and neither can we see the time-to-come quite close to us, and thus it is that meekness can be without anxiety even about the morrow. And is not this the bearing lightly the heavy burden of time, of time-to-come? So when one born a slave, as the Apostle earnestly exhorts him[1] (for Christ did not come to banish slavery, though that will follow, and does follow) when he is not anxious because of it, and only if chance offers will be free, then he is bearing lightly the heavy burden. How heavy the burden is, he, the unfortunate, best knows himself, and human sympathy knows too. If he should sigh beneath the burden, as humanity does with him, then he is bearing the burden heavily. If he accepts his fate with patience, and patiently hopes for freedom, still he is not bearing his burden lightly. But the meek one who has had the courage to believe sincerely in the freedom of the spirit, he is bearing lightly the heavy burden; he neither gives up hope of freedom, nor does he look for it. That which is properly called the decisive question, the question of freedom, the question which for a slave must surely be called a vital question, to be or not to be, that destroying or life-giving question is by the meek man treated as lightly as if it did not affect him, and yet again as lightly as if in a sense it did affect him, for he says: I am not anxious because I was born a slave, but if I may be free I would choose it rather.

[1] 1 Cor. vii. 21.

To gnaw one's bonds is to bear them heavily, to scoff at one's bonds is also to bear them heavily, to bear the bonds patiently is still not bearing them lightly, but, having been born a slave, to bear the bondage of slavery as a free man can wear a chain of honour—that is bearing it lightly.

And so is meekness ever. As at times we are amazed what thrift can do with pence, so is the spirit that strives not, strong to make adversities—and that means what is heavy—light. As a faithless man in timid self-restraint will scarcely dare to tread the ground, will dare neither to deny nor to affirm anything, lest he should go too far, even so the meek man is under the restraint of the eternal; yet he is not timid but, on the contrary, of a cheerful courage; he is not faithless but believing. He breathes the free and healthy atmosphere of faith, and still his courage is so effortless that the load looks like nothing at all that he has to carry. It is a fact that every state of mind projects itself, transforming its task into likeness with itself. We may not say: Where there is great danger there is always found a man of courage. But we may say the converse: Where there is a man of courage there is sure to be great danger, for he needs it, he craves for it, it is a necessity of the instinct of self-preservation for the courage of the courageous man. The problem becomes a different problem in relation to whatever person solves it. The same danger which may be conquered by the faint-hearted becomes plainly greater when it is a courageous man who conquers it. The same injustice the complacent man endures becomes plainly greater when it is an upright man who endures it. The same leap that is made by a fugitive driven by fear becomes plainly greater when a dancer performs it with ease. And thus does courage[1] make the danger great and conquer it: generosity[1] makes the injury mean and rises above it: patience[1] makes the burden heavy and bears it: but meekness[1] makes the burden light, and bears it lightly.

Meekness is therefore, speaking humanly, an unrewarded virtue. For meekness passes by so quietly that none is aware

[1] *mod*; hoï-*mod*; taal-*mod*; sagt-*mod*.

of the hard part it is playing; not even he who lays the burden on the meek one really comes to know of it. Courage does reap its reward by visible victory, generosity by the gleam of pride, patience by the evidence of suffering, but meekness is not to be recognised. Thus does a meek slave hide by his meekness the injustice of his master, for it appears in fact as if the slave was very fortunate with his master, and so he is—through his meekness! Therefore if a traveller should see how slaves are groaning in the oppression of their bondage, his sympathy would be aroused and he would give a passionate account of the horror of slavery; but towards the meek bondsman his attention would not be drawn and he might even believe the master was the upright man. Thus too, when a passive woman meekly bears with all the difficult behaviour of her husband, his whims, his wrongs, perhaps unfaithfulness, does it not seem —but what is the good of speaking of how it seems? for it cannot be seen. If she bears patiently, then perhaps it can be seen. But somewhere or other, wherever such a meek woman lives, we see only a happy married life, we see only a beloved husband, and a wife who is happy in her home, happy in her husband. And truly she is blest, if not happy, in her husband, yet blest she is because of her meekness.

"Learn of me, for I am meek and lowly of heart." In truth Christ was meek. Had he not been the Meek One, then neither had he been what he said of himself that he was. But had he not been the Meek One, neither would he have suffered so much, for then the world itself would have shuddered at the wrong done him; but his meekness concealed the guilt of the world. He asserted not his cause; he pled not his innocence; he spake not of how they sinned against him; not by one word did he point to that most shameful guilt; even at the last moment he said: Father, forgive them, for they know not what they do. Does not his meekness in this conceal their crime, since by his speaking of it thus it becomes so very much less than it is; while yet in another sense it becomes even more fearful, being a sin against meekness! When Peter had denied him thrice and Christ did no more than meekly look at him is not the effect of meekness to conceal the guilt of Peter and to make of it something far less! Hear the wail that is in the mere words: thrice to deny his Lord, at the very moment when he is being betrayed, in the power of his enemies, scorned, and mocked! Thou dost shudder to learn of it, not by any description of it, but merely by hearing it told. But the meekness of Christ prevents our learning how deep was that fall.

This meekness we have to learn from him, and this meekness is the most distinctive mark of a Christian. "Whosoever shall smite thee on thy right cheek, turn to him the other also."[1] It is not meekness to refrain from striking back, it is not meekness to submit to the wrong and take it for what it is, but it is meekness to offer the left cheek. Generosity also endures the wrong, but so as to make it seem a greater wrong by rising above it; patience also endures the wrong, but does not make it less than it is; meekness alone makes the wrong less, for when anyone will not take a thing for what it is, and what he takes is an injustice, a wrong done to him, an outrage, then he truly makes the wrong less. Let it happen before our eyes. At the moment the first blow is struck, thou must give all thy heed—is it not so?—to the wrong that is done; it is seen in the generous man, and it is seen in the patient man, but as the meek man in his quiet way offers the other cheek thou art hindered from giving heed to the wrong, so lightly he bears it that almost thine anger against the aggressor is lessened. It is not meekness, that thou dost forgive thine enemy, but the seventy times seven—that is the meekness! Or rather *this*: that the meek man is so eager to forgive that it almost seems as if it were he who stood in need of being forgiven, as if the meek man, knowing in his humility how heaven's forgiveness towards himself depends on his forgiving, were indeed yearning to forgive his enemy.

So meekness bears the heavy burden lightly, and the burden of a wrong inflicted, so lightly that it seems as if the offence

[1] Matt. v. 39.

of the guilty one were lessened. Such meekness is unknown to paganism. In a Christian view it has one splendid property in that it has no reward on earth, and yet another splendid property: great is its reward in heaven!

And now we have spoken of how a Christian bears the heavy burden lightly, how he is not distinguished from other men by being excused the burden, but a Christian through bearing it lightly. One who bears the kindly yoke, one who though heavy-laden is bearing a burden that is light—he is a Christian!

But when Christ speaks of the light burden and when he says *my* burden, then we may understand by this a quite special burden he has laid upon his followers. Truly he has bid them bear human burdens lightly, but a light burden also which is proper to Christians. What is this burden? First let us ask this question: Which of all burdens is the heaviest? Surely that of the consciousness of sin, on this we should all be agreed. *But one who takes away the consciousness of sin and gives instead a consciousness of pardon*—he takes away indeed the heavy burden and gives the light one in its place.

But how! A burden, and we may call it light? Yea. If any man will not understand that forgiveness too is truly a burden to be borne, albeit a light one, then he is taking forgiveness in vain. Forgiveness is not to be earned, it is not as heavy as that; but neither is it to be taken in vain, for neither is it so light. Forgiveness is not to be paid for, it is not as costly as that—for it cannot be paid for; but neither is it to be taken as if it were nothing, it is too costly for that.

See how here also it is proper to meekness to believe, to bear the light burden of forgiveness, to bear the joy of forgiveness. For flesh and blood it must be difficult to bear the light burden; but if the light burden becomes hard to bear it is because of a rebellious spirit, that will not believe. But if, on the other hand, the light burden becomes so light that it cannot be called a burden at all then it is because of lightmindedness that has taken it in vain. Forgiveness, or reconciliation with God, is a burden light to bear, and yet it is like a light burden for meekness precisely because for flesh and blood it is the heaviest burden, still heavier than the consciousness of sin, for it is a stumbling block. Therefore as the Christian man is ever to be known by his meekness, so the essentially Christian fact corresponds exactly, for only in meekness can it be believed. Every extreme, whether heavy-hearted or light-hearted, is the immediate evidence that faith is not sincerely held. For Christ did not come into the world to make life easy in the light-hearted sense, nor yet to make it heavy in the sense of a mournful heart, but to lay the light burden on the believer. The light-hearted would allow all to be forgotten—he believes in vain. The mournful heart would allow nothing to be forgotten —he believes in vain. But he who believes, believes that all is forgotten, only in this wise, that he is bearing a light burden —for is he not bearing the memory that he has been forgiven? The light-hearted would let even that memory be forgotten— all is forgotten and forgiven! But Faith says: All is forgotten; remember that it has been forgiven. One may forget indeed in many ways. One may forget, because one gets something else to think about. One may forget thoughtlessly and frivolously. One may consider that all has been forgotten because one has oneself forgotten—but the eternal righteousness can forget and will forget only in one way, through forgiveness. And so the believer himself must not forget, but on the contrary must constantly remind himself, that all has been forgiven him. The mournful heart will not forget, for he will not remember he has been forgiven, and he will bear in mind the guilt; therefore he cannot believe. But *out* of forgiveness a new life should spring forth in the believer, therefore the forgiveness is not to be forgotten. No longer is the law our schoolmaster to bring us to Christ, but forgiveness through Christ is the gentle chastener that has not in its heart to remind us of what has been forgotten, and yet so far reminds us of it as to say: Do not forget that it has been forgiven. It has not been forgotten simply, but it has been forgotten in forgiveness. Every time thou dost remember the forgiveness, then it is forgotten, but when thou dost forget the forgiveness, then is it not forgotten, for then forgiveness has been forfeited.

Is this not truly a light burden? If, my hearer, thou knowest how otherwise to interpret it then interpret it to me. For I know no other sense than this simple one, of faith, which is nevertheless linked to a difficult way of speaking, for it is always a difficult way of speaking that brings together two such different words as light and—burden! It is a difficult way of speaking, but human life, itself, also has its difficulties. Yet the difficult way of speaking tends to understanding, and the difficulties of life are bearable, yea, by a Christian are to be borne lightly—since for him the yoke is good and the burden light.

III

CHILDREN we come to know best when we watch them at their play, and young men when we overhear their wishes—what they would like to be in the world, or what they would like to get from the world. For whereas the making of a choice is the serious part of life, and even the foolish choice at which one can scarce refrain from smiling is still a serious matter—pathetically serious; wishing, on the other hand, is like guessing—an amusement. Nevertheless it is from his wish that we come to know the young man best. For a choice, like anything actual, shares many of the limitations of the actual. Perhaps the conditions of the choice are restricted, or else he who chooses is confined by the many factors that determine all actuality, and is at the same time cramped and supported by innumerable considerations. In his wish, on the other hand, everything suits itself to the youth. The illusion of possibility is entirely at his service, and just for that reason lures him into disclosing his inmost soul. In desire he is utterly himself, and his desire is the exact reflection of his inmost being. And that in his desire the youth should thus disclose his inmost being is quite an innocent thing, and may even be useful to him in teaching him to know himself and recognise his immaturity. The danger is when later on a desire that is hidden turns traitor against him. For a wish that is really open does no harm, but being hidden it can easily prove treacherous.

If we should suppose a group of young men, every one wishing, then through their wishes we could see how far there was any greater depth of soul in any of them. For there is no mirror so true as desire, and though at times even a mirror does flatter one who regards himself therein, and shows him different from what he actually is, yet we are bound to say of desire that while by opening up the possible it too may flatter him, yet it does coax him to appear exactly what he is, coaxes him to an absolute likeness of himself. But we shall not pursue this further, but only suppose that among those young men there was one of them who said: Nay, I wish for neither power nor wealth, nor honour, nor the joy of love; all I wish for is conflict and danger, hardship and suffering; this alone inspires my soul. Thus he spake, and whatever is said by an unspoilt youth, we may be certain that it holds some wisdom, if only we understand it somewhat differently from the way he said it.

And so there was a youth who would suffer in the world. Yet did he, we may ask, express quite accurately his desire, for obviously he wanted not merely to suffer, but quite on the contrary he wanted to strive? That there was depth in his soul we shall not deny him. He would not spend his life for enjoyment like a drone. He would not shine in an excellence achieved in sleep, nor sit in state like a coward and a sluggard, holding a position won by favour. He fain would strive, yet strive not for the sake of honour, gain, or power, but strive for the sake of striving. But strife for striving's sake is by no means the same as suffering. Indeed, it is the very opposite and yet, let us note, it is that kind of opposite which has the greatest resemblance. While another man wants to know that he is the stronger, and seeks the proof of it that is found in the honour and reputation and power won by striving, this young man forever would renew his pride of spirit in being the stronger in the contest, by continuing to strive for the sake of striving. It were no satisfaction to him to settle down and take his ease; the yearning of his soul were too great for that; and he would pay no heed if told the contest now was over. Nay, as the spirit of the bow-string yearns for this alone: that it should be strained in the tension of the fight; and grieves for this alone: to be unstrung and hung away, no matter how many its victories; thus and not otherwise would he too live and die, in the strife, and be found in the day of battle first in the tenseness of the struggle and the last to leave it, even in the maelstrom of the fight.

It was therefore a misunderstanding, a self-deception, a delusion, when the young man uttered those wise words, *to suffer*, to desire to suffer. Should one repeat his words, and say to him, In truth you chose aright, and then unfold what lay therein, it might well be that that young man with the fighting spirit, who in his wish had challenged the world to combat, would lose his courage, and he might, instead of falling in the fight, sink underneath his suffering. For oh, this willing to suffer, this choice of suffering, is a wish that has never been found in any mortal's heart; and any who thinks it has, he but deceives himself.

To grasp the thought of suffering, and the message of joy in suffering, to endure suffering and truly find good in it, to choose to suffer and believe that this is true wisdom unto blessedness, a man requires the guidance of God. The natural man can never dream of wishing it. There must first have been the deepest change in a man before he can believe in this mystery of sufferings; he must first have been deeply moved, and then have been willing to learn from him who alone went out into the world on set purpose to suffer, making the choice, and the demand, that he should suffer. He went out into the world, but he did not go as a young man goes from his father's house, he went out from the Father in heaven, and gave up the glory he had from the foundation of the world, yea, from eternity his choice was free, and he came to the world—in order to suffer!

Of him, of the Lord Jesus Christ, it is said that *"Though he was a Son, yet learned he obedience by the things which he suffered."*[1] And it is these words we shall take for our consideration, dwelling on this, that while nobody as he is by nature can desire sufferings, yet we may rejoice to know

THAT THE SCHOOL OF SUFFERINGS FITS US FOR ETERNITY.

When it is said of anybody: He learned from what he suffered,

[1] Heb. v. 8.

the phrase holds both what attracts and what repels. What attracts is that he learned. For people are not minded to refuse to learn; on the contrary, they are eager to learn, and especially eager to *have learned* something. They would preferably like to learn everything *very quickly*, but should it be that some effort is necessary, then they are also willing to make the effort. When, however, it is a question of learning but a *little*, and of learning it *slowly*—though it mean learning it by heart as well —then from the very outset they are impatient, and when a long time passes, grow—to use a sardonic turn of words— heartily impatient. But if suffering is to be the schoolmaster and to be the lesson taught, then they lose the desire to learn altogether; then in their own opinion they are wise enough already, wise enough too to see that you can pay too dearly for wisdom; and this is because they were not capable of making a sound judgment immediately, thinking through suffering, and understanding the good that it might do them. For when the suffering is not so great, not so serious, not so heavy, not so difficult, but that the mind can apprehend at once the benefit of it, then that suffering is not a teaching, but what is accompanied by hardship and by suffering is a teaching—and that is quite a different matter. People are eager enough to learn, and, when they hear of a great teacher, make haste to go to him, and the incitement to learn is quickly stirred, and they are eager to pay for teaching both with money and with admiration; indeed, they vie with one another to get to him, for it flatters vanity to have been taught—by one whom they admire!—by him whom they pay with money and admiration, at the same time turning him into money and causing themselves to be paid because they have been taught—by him whom they admire! But if the teacher will not deceive them, and will accept neither their money nor their admiration, if he knows one truth alone and will know none but that, a truth of which he himself is far from being the discoverer, and in which he himself is no more than a learner, namely, that it is through sufferings, in sufferings borne by himself alone, and from sufferings, that a man by the help of God must learn that which is high above all else, then they become impatient and tend to grow bitter towards the teacher. The same young man who had nothing but admiration for the teacher, and wanted only to be his first disciple, so that he might proclaim the praise of him he admired, grows bitter when he hears that suffering is to be the teacher to whom all must be referred. Strange, is it not, that the young man in his eager admiration should have a need of the teacher that he might be deceived by him, and yet is provoked to anger at the idea that he can do without the teacher and can be in the truth through the help of sufferings! Strange, is it not, that the good most coveted in the world is independence, and yet there is hardly anybody who covets the only way that really leads to it—sufferings! Men are eager to learn something, to learn something by which they might become something, to learn something from which they might derive good, or to learn something of which it might be said by the learner that he has great knowledge because he knows it. But when it is a question of learning to know oneself through sufferings then men lose courage and the capacity to understand, then, from their own viewpoint, it is easy to see that the result is out of proportion to the hardship it involves. Alas! it might well be said that instead of learning something every man needs first to learn what is the most important thing to learn. And this first, basic lesson, more fundamental than any other, which is precisely what sufferings teach us, is the one that is coveted least of all.

"*He learned obedience by the things which he suffered.*" If thou wilt, my hearer, imagine some quite lowly one; he lives remote, his powers are very slight—of such a one would not the world say: What should he be able to learn? And yet, there is one thing yet that he can learn, he can learn obedience; yea, even were his powers still slighter than they are, yet, there is one thing yet that he can learn, he can learn obedience. But why indeed is it so hard to learn obedience, but that one first must learn that obedience is indeed worth learning, and that obedience is so far from being what we busy men imagine to be waste of time, that it is precisely everlasting gain. Why is this so difficult to believe? Because to obey is so difficult. And why is it so difficult to learn to obey? Because first we must learn that the lesson is of eternal worth. All the knowledge that is allied with curiosity, with the desire to know, with natural ability, with selfish passion, all the knowledge which the natural man is instinctively aware is worth the learning, is also in the last analysis for the most part easy to learn, and that which matters first and last is aptitude. Thus men are willing enough when it is a question of *acquiring knowledge*, but when it is a question of *coming to know* through sufferings, then it becomes so hard that on the one hand aptitude does not help, but neither, on the other hand, is any excluded, though aptitude be sadly lacking. The lowliest, most simple-minded, most forsaken of men, given up by all the teachers, is surely not given up by heaven, and he can learn obedience just as well as any other.

This is the one whom thou didst have in mind at the outset, O my hearer,—the least of men. But now think, that he of whom the Holy Scripture says, that he learned obedience by the things which he suffered, he it was who was with the Father from eternity, he it was who came in the fulness of time, he it was who finished what the Father had begun, he, who perfected creation and transformed the fashion of the world. And of him the Holy Scripture speaks as it does of the least of men, nothing is said about who he was, about what he was, about what he could do, about what he accomplished, nothing about his work, which is above all human thought, it is said only that he learned obedience by the things which he suffered. Ah! the one who knew all, whose thought comprehends all, who needed not to come to the knowledge of anything, because what he knows not does not even exist, of him is it said that he learned obedience by the things which he suffered.

Christ *learned* obedience. Indeed from eternity his will

accorded with the Father's, and he freely chose the Father's will. But when, as in the fulness of the time, he came, thereupon he learned obedience by the things which he suffered—which he suffered when he came unto his own, and they did not know him, when he went about here in the humble guise of a servant, and bore the weight of God's eternal plan, and his words were spoken as if in vain, when he, in whom alone there is salvation, was in the world as something superfluous, when he accomplished nothing—nothing!—when nobody heeded him, or, what was even harder still, when he aroused the worthless interest of a vagrant curiosity. Oh, even when evil rose up against him, in fury unrestrained, and dragged him away, the Holy One, to death, even that was not so much to shudder at, as when he was an object of men's curiosity, when the Saviour of the world could not accomplish anything in this lost world, except to gather the idly curious about him, so that the craftsman left his work to gaze after him, and the merchant ran out from his stall, and even one who hurried past would glance behind him curiously. Even the vinegar was not a drink more sour for the Holy One, than the vacuous interest taken by the idle, and the revolting tribute curiosity accorded him who is the Truth! Even rash sin against the Holy One was not more bitter than to be taken lightly by the curious!

Yea, he learned obedience by the things which he suffered—which he suffered when he, who is the Lord of bliss, was as a curse for everyone approaching him, and for everyone who fled him a sorrow while he lived; a sorrow for those few who loved him, since he must draw them out with him into the most dread decisions, since for a mother he must be the sword to pierce her heart, for his disciples, love crucified; a sorrow for the hesitating who, deep down, in the impenetrable secret of desire, understood perhaps that his words were true, but dared not join themselves to him, wherefore also they retained in their souls a goad, an inner discord, the painful evidence of being his contemporaries; a sorrow for the wicked, since by his purity and holiness he must reveal their hearts' thought to them, making them guiltier than before. Oh, grievous suffering, that as the Saviour of the world he must become a stumbling-stone!

He learned obedience by the things which he suffered—which he suffered when indeed of his own choice he sought, but also was, as it were, compelled to seek, the fellowship despised of publicans and sinners, when none would dare acknowledge his acquaintance, when the curious wagged their heads suspiciously, and in their vanity the shrewd would scoff and say: The fool! and sympathy commiserating shrugged its shoulders; when pride regarded him with criticism as he came, and cowardice slunk aside; when every estimable person fled, that he might not be suspected, when even one of the nobler sort would make the circumstances of his dealings with him ambiguous, so that he might not lose too much by them, when he who had drawn back in time thought himself fortunate, when none considered he had any duty towards him, but counted everything permissible that would afford protection from him, when even his dear disciple uttered a denial.

He learned obedience by the things which he suffered—which he suffered when Pilate said, Behold the man.[1] It is not the wild mob, not the deluded raging multitude, that cries out thus in mockery; nay, it is one who wears the purple, an exalted personage, who thus speaks to despise him. Judas sold him for thirty shekels; Pilate would sell him at a still better bargain, make of him a miserable wretch, poor object fit to satisfy a raging mob's contempt.

And thus the whole of his earthly life was the deepest suffering, deep as no mortal's ever can be, deep as no mortal can imagine it, deeper than language can express. But for that very reason it was also in the highest sense such suffering, that from it could be learned obedience. For when one who is guilty suffers, not only has he no reason—as none ever has any reason—but there is not even the appearance of *excuse*,

[1] John xix. 5. Danish version: "See! what a man!"

for losing faith in God. As little is there any merit when he suffers his punishment with patience. On the other hand, when one suffers who is innocent, then there is a chance to learn; the opportunity is there, but it does not follow that it is obedience that is learned. But Christ did learn *obedience* by the things which he suffered. He said: "O my Father, if it be possible, let this cup pass from me: nevertheless not as I will, but as thou wilt."[1] So to have spoken is the first phase of his obedience, an l that then he drained the bitter cup is the second phase of his obedience. If without speaking thus he had drained the bitter cup, his obedience had not been perfect. To obedience belongs—and this comes first—the question that is a prayer and the prayer that is a question: if it be the Father's will, if it be not possible to be otherwise. And thus was his life obedience, obedience unto death, unto death on the cross. He, who was the truth, the way, and the life, he, who needed not to learn anything, yet learned one thing—he learned obedience! So close is the relation of obedience to the eternal truth, that he, who is the truth, yet learns obedience!

And now, if we could say that obedience followed as a matter of course from suffering, then we might expect to find a man with the courage to choose suffering, one who, when suffering befell, had the courage to reckon he was fortunate. Ah, but it is not thus; learning does not come about so easily. Suffering itself is, from a human point of view, the first danger, but the second danger, which is still more terrible, is that we should not learn obedience. Suffering is a lesson full of danger; for, if we do not learn obedience—ah, then it is as terrible as if the most efficacious of medicines had the wrong kind of effect! In such danger man needs help: he needs the help of God; else he learns not obedience. And if he does not learn obedience then he may learn the worst corruption—learn a cowardly hopelessness, learn a quenching of the spirit, learn to damp down whatever fire of nobility is in him, learn perverseness and despair. But just because the lesson of sufferings

[1] Matt. xxvi. 39.

is so dangerous, therefore we say, quite rightly, that in this school we are fitted for eternity; for in no other school is there such a danger, but neither is there such a prize: the greatest danger and the greatest prize—but the greatest of prizes is eternity.

It is true that a man may learn much without ever coming into relation with the eternal. For when in his learning he looks back upon himself, it is true that he may acquire much knowledge, and yet in spite of all this knowledge he may be, and may continue to be, to himself a mystery, one unknown. As the wind drives mighty ships although the wind has no self-understanding, and as the river drives the wheel, although the river has no self-understanding, so may a man perform astonishing feats and comprehend a vast amount of knowledge, and yet have no understanding of himself. But suffering directs a man to look within. If it succeeds, the man will not despairingly resist, nor seek, for the sake of forgetfulness, to plunge into the distraction of the world, into astounding enterprises, into an all-embracing and undifferentiated knowledge—if it succeeds, then there, within him, is the beginning of his learning. And as, in another connection, it is said of school-life, that it must be kept remote from contact with the world, hedged-about, sheltered, quiet, and retired, so is it truly said of this school of sufferings. For it is in the inner life that suffering teaches, and God hears us our lesson, and obedience is the test that is exacted. It is true that the suffering often comes from without, but it is when suffering has been received within that the lesson first begins. Many sufferings may come storming in upon a man, and a man may succeed in repelling the charge—so to speak—and may keep himself safe and sound. That is to say, he may succeed in preventing himself from beginning with the lesson of suffering. And worldly wisdom knows of many remedies for sufferings, but all these remedies have this unhappy feature, that they save the body but destroy the soul. And worldly wisdom knows of many invigorating cures for those who suffer, but all these invigorating cures have this unhappy feature, that they fortify the body, but vex the spirit. And worldly wisdom knows how to give, in sufferings, a passionate desire for life, but in sufferings it is only inwardness that wins eternity.

When anyone is suffering and would learn from what he suffers, *then it is always something about himself and about his relation to God, and nothing else, that he comes to know, and this is the token that he is being fitted for eternity.* Yea, no doubt a man in the course of his sufferings comes to know much about the world, how false and treacherous it is, and much more of the same sort, but all such knowledge is not the lesson of sufferings. Nay, just as we say that a child is to be weaned when he is allowed no longer to be, as it were, one with the mother, so is a man, in the deepest sense, to be weaned by sufferings, weaned from the world and what is of the world, from love of it, and from bitterness towards it, in order that he may study for eternity. And therefore is the school of sufferings a "dying-unto", spaced into the quiet lesson hours of "dying-unto"—the lesson-hour is always quiet in this school; attention is not drawn away by the number of the subjects for instruction, for here but the one thing needful is taught; attention is not disturbed by fellow-pupils, for here the pupil is alone with God. There is no question of the capacity of the teacher to instruct, for God is the Teacher. Only this one thing is taught: obedience. Without sufferings none can learn obedience, for suffering is the very guarantee that our devotion is not our own self-will. But he who learns obedience learns all. We say, moreover, that he who would learn to command must learn to obey, and this is very true, but there is a yet more splendid lesson in the learning of obedience in the school of sufferings: to let God command, to leave to God to ordain. What, however, is the whole of eternal truth other than this: that God ordains! And what is obedience other than to let God ordain! And what other relation can there be, or what agreement, between the temporal and the eternal than: that God ordains, and to leave to God to ordain! And where, but in the school of sufferings, is this lesson taught—when the child is weaned, and self-will dies, and the sufferer painfully learns, first, that in spite of all, it is God who ordains, and then goes on to learn in glad obedience, to leave to God to ordain!

All a man knows about the eternal is first of all summed up in this: it is God who ordains; for what more he comes to know concerns *how* God has ordained, ordains, or will ordain. But in the language of obedience this eternal truth is rendered thus: to leave to God to ordain. It is altogether the same, except that in this obedience there is to be heard a humble resignation that utters an assenting, confident Yea! If the fear of God be the beginning of wisdom, then the learning of obedience is the perfecting of wisdom; it is our progress in wisdom, fitting us for eternity. Yea, if ever in the discipline of sufferings thou hast submitted with a perfect, absolute obedience, then truly hast thou felt the eternal present in thee, and known the quiet and the rest of the eternal. For there is quiet where the eternal is, but unrest where the eternal is not. There is unrest in the world, but especially in man's soul is unrest, when the eternal is not in it, and he is but "full of tossings to and fro."[1] But if distractions, that are supposed to dispel unrest, increase it, so sufferings, that are supposed to increase it, dispel it. The stern reality of our sufferings in the first instance lies in the fact that they are a discipline and make our unrest greater, but if one who suffers is willing to learn then is he being fitted for eternity.

For the finding of rest is our fitting for eternity. In the long run there is nothing but this in which rest can be found: to let God rule in everything; whatever more one may get to know is a matter of *how* the will of God has ruled. There is a reconciliation for the contrite heart, and the thought holds rest, but none may find rest in this eternal thought who rests not first in the thought of obedience, namely, that God must rule in all: for reconciliation itself is the rule of God for the

[1] Job vii. 4.

salvation of man. The guilt has been atoned for, and for the repentant the thought of it holds rest, but none may find rest in this eternal thought who rests not first in the thought that God must rule in all; for atonement itself is the rule of God from all eternity. God will in his mercy receive thee, and the thought of it holds rest, but thou mayst not find rest in this abiding thought unless thou rest in the thought that God must rule in all. Else would the grace of God be earned by thee, whereas it is of the gift of God that we both will and do, of his gift is the growth, and of his gift the perfecting, and all thine own endeavour could not accomplish it, for it adds not one cubit to thy stature, not an inch, and all thy taking of thought could not accomplish it, for it but vexes the spirit and prevents thee from growing. But faith, and faith's obedience in suffering, makes for growth; for all the working of faith tends to do away with self-will and selfishness, so that God may truly be admitted, and then allowed to rule in all things. The more one suffers, if at the same time one learns from suffering, the more is all selfishness taken away; it is uprooted, and obedience comes in instead, as the good soil in which eternity can strike its roots. Thou canst not seize the eternal, thou canst but receive it; but thou canst not receive what is thine own, only what is another's; and yet this thou canst not properly receive unless he give it thee; if, however, he will give it thee, then to receive it is to make it more intrinsically thine. But in relation to God to receive is to obey, and in obedience is rest. There is rest in the eternal, and this is the eternal truth. But the eternal can rest only in obedience, and this is the eternal truth for thee.

Hence, whenever unrest comes, it is because thou art not willing to obey; but towards obedience suffering is thine aid. When there is suffering therefore, but obedience in suffering as well, then art thou being fitted for eternity, then is there no impatient straining in thy soul, no unrest, whether of sin or of sorrow. As the Cherubim stood with a flaming sword that Adam might not return to Paradise, so suffering is the angel who saves thee, that thou mayst not return again to the world. Suffering both is the school, and will keep thee in school, that thou mayst be made fit for eternity. And, as one of the ancient prophets has said, the idolater carries his god, but the true God carries them that believe in him;[1] so the obedience that would let God rule in all things is itself true knowledge of the only true God—but what else then is our being fitted for eternity! While the idolater, whatever his idol may be, in disobedience and self-will drags on to death, determined to carry his god, so he who has learned obedience by the things which he suffered is lightly carried by God—lightly, as only he is lightly borne who is being fitted for eternity.

The school of sufferings fits us for eternity. We speak at different times in different ways of schooling, saying of one school that it fits us for science, of another, for art, of a third, for a certain position in life, and so on. And by this we imply that school has its time, but there will also come a time when one shall benefit from what one learned at school. When, however, the school of sufferings seems to the sufferer to be long drawn out, then perhaps he murmurs with a sigh, This schooltime never ends! and no doubt thinks that this complaint implies the heaviest load of suffering.

But is it so indeed? Men of science take for granted that the length of time required for growth is in direct proportion to a creature's worth. The lowest forms of animal life are born in a moment, and almost the same moment die. The lower animals grow very quickly. Man among all the creatures grows the slowest, and this to men of science is evidence direct that he is of the highest worth. And in the same manner do we speak of schooling. One whose lot it is to serve in a humble capacity goes but for a short time to school, but one whose lot is something higher, he goes to school for a long time. And so the length of time at school is in direct proportion to the importance of what one is going to be. If then the school of

[1] Isa. xlvi. 1-7.

sufferings lasts a whole lifetime, it is the very evidence that this school must be fitting us for what is highest, yea, that it alone fits for eternity, for no other schooltime lasts so long. It is true that if temporal wisdom were to reckon that one must go to school with it for a whole lifetime, then the pupil quite rightly might become impatient and say: When at last am I to have the benefit of what I have learned in this school? Only eternity can justify, for itself and for the pupil, the turning into a schooltime of his whole life. But if eternity is to keep school, then it must be truly the finest school; the finest, however, is just the one that lasts the longest. As when sometimes a master says to the young pupil who too soon finds schooltime far too long: Indeed thou must not be impatient, a whole life lies before thee—so does eternity, with greater justification and with more conviction, say to one who suffers: Indeed thou must not be impatient, there is time enough, there is eternity. And when eternity speaks there is no guile found in its mouth, as in the master's well-meaning words— for how can the master answer for the length of time that may lie before the youth! But eternity must know of its own existence, and when it shall be, and so indeed there is time enough.

The longest schooltime fits for what is highest; the school which lasts just as long as time can fit us only for eternity. The school for life shows its results in time, but the lifelong school of sufferings fits us for eternity. It fits us for eternity, and it is known by this as well, that whereas in any other schooltime we grow older by going to school, and this is just what should be, in eternity's school one becomes younger, and this is just what should be. Eternal life rejuvenates. Ought there not then to be time enough for the pupil to derive both benefit and joy from what he has learned? For what creates impatience with the schooltime that is far too prolonged but this, that with every year one grows older, and hence has good reason to fear that the time of going to school will last too long! But when with every year one becomes younger! Could there be a more comforting thought! It has the power to make of the longest schooltime the shortest! For if the shortest schooltime has lasted but one year, yet the pupil is one year older; whereas when the longest schooltime has lasted seventy years, and every year the pupil has grown younger, then plainly this schooltime is yet shorter than the shortest.

No doubt it is a very beautiful and a blessed and an edifying thought that eternal life is a renewing of youth. And yet I will not elaborate further upon it, because to my mind it is so beautiful as to be almost dangerous, and it can ever so easily lead to disappointment. For just in revealing itself in all its beauty to a man, it may, instead of giving him the impetus to strive, take hold of his imagination, as if the renewal were effected by an act of magic, as if, in other words, the renewal did not require any length of time. Indeed a man must have learned a very great deal, and learned it very thoroughly, in the school of suffering, before, to his true edification, he dares to let his mind dwell on such an elevated thought. If with reference to other matters it is true that one must creep before one can walk, then here it is true to say that one must walk before one begins to fly. And this thought flies as high as to eternity. Therefore I ever prefer to speak of what is more lowly, of the slow and heavy going of one who begins, for to speak so cannot mislead anybody; while, on the other hand, if anyone has advanced so far that it is for his genuine edification and furtherance on his way when he can find refreshment in this thought of the renewal of his youth, then such a one needs not any to speak to him, and least of all me, for I on the contrary have real need to learn of him.

But although I shall not speak any more myself about this, yet in conclusion, and in order that this discourse may quite achieve the end it had in view—the JOY we may find in the thought, that the school of sufferings fits us for eternity—I would bring to notice what one of the earliest teachers of the Church, one of the apostolic fathers,[1] has represented so beautifully. In the part of his writings called *The Visions*, he tells

---

[1] Hermas.

how God granted him three visions. Besides the significance in the substance of them these had this remarkable feature, that the person who showed them to him and explained them was a very old woman the first time, the second time she was younger, and looked happier, but still had the old woman's hair and her wrinkled skin, the third time she was young, happy and yet grave, as is the youth of eternity. And then he himself gives a more detailed explanation of the matter, but among other things he adds this too: "They whose penance is sincere shall grow younger." So does he put a restraint on this most mighty thought, lest it should become such a soaring fantasy that the learner not only becomes no younger, but, even worse than becoming older, becomes a dupe. And so also does this our discourse apply restraint; for it is only the school of suffering that fits us for eternity. If anything of this sort is to happen to a man then it must happen to him in the school of suffering.

But that is why the Joy in the thought still remains; it remains in the end, as here it is, at the end: that no schooling lasts as long as that of suffering; that none else therefore fits us for eternity; and that in eternity's school it may come to pass that the learner be renewed in youth. Not knowledge, not a well-stored mind, nay, nothing without suffering, when from suffering a man learns obedience, fits for eternity—just as certainly as he who was and who is the Truth, he who knew all, yet learned one thing, and nothing else, learned obedience by the things which he suffered. Were it possible that a man should learn obedience to God apart from sufferings, then Christ, as man, had not needed to learn it from sufferings. It was human obedience that he learned from sufferings, for the eternal accord of his will with that of the Father is certainly not obedience. Obedience belongs to his humiliation, as it is written; "he humbled himself and became obedient".[1] But this, this obedience of his, is just what it means to be man, and so it is true of a man in relation to God that obedience is

[1] Phil. ii. 8.

learned only from sufferings; and if this is true of the pure how much more of the sinful man! Only suffering fits for eternity; for eternity resides in faith, but faith resides in obedience, and obedience resides in suffering. There is no obedience apart from suffering, no faith apart from obedience, no eternity apart from faith. In suffering obedience is obedience, in obedience faith is faith, in faith eternity is eternity.

IV

WHEN we hear a beautiful saying, an edifying saying, a moving saying, a saying that makes us exclaim, "How true!" then we would fain enquire the author of it, and when, and in what circumstances, he uttered it; that is to say, we want to find out to what degree so true a saying may have been the truth also for him who said it, as we fervently hope it was, not for our own sakes only but for his as well.

For a brilliant saying that is void of truth is "like a tree that bears lovely fruit in vain",[1] and a true saying that is not true in the speaker is altogether as lacking in inspiration as a blessing that curses him who gives it. But a true saying that has its truth in the speaker is the most perfect example of apples of gold in baskets of silver.[2] As if what is said were the thing of supreme value, wherefore it is likened to an apple of gold, whereas the speaker is but the precious vessel of fine silver, wherein what is true is fittingly set in the truth. And in this sense indeed the saying is of the greater value, that it goes out into the world and others make it their own; which means, not that they have said it, but only that they have acted on it; yet every time they thus put it to the proof they are humbly bringing to mind again its first fine setting.

And so when a king[3] says of the riches and the power and the glory of this world that it is altogether vanity, then we are glad that the speaker is a king. For he must surely have had the opportunity to know from his experience. He is not like one whom such things seen from a distance dazzle with the eagerness of desire, for he has seen them close at hand. When the man who possessed such plenty that it might have seemed to be all, but by that same token had also lost all, when he says, Blessèd be the name of the Lord![4]—then we are reassured and gladdened by it, for he was the one who underwent the trial.

[1] Wisdom x. 7.   [2] Prov. xxv. 11 (R.V.).   [3] Eccles.   [4] Job i. 21.

Thus are many excellent sayings cherished, with a remembrance of the speakers of them, and among these there is a thief also. This cannot repel us; on the contrary, we should miss him if there were not such a one. For in the realm of truth no distinction is made between a king and a thief; there the only question is whether what he said is true and whether it was the truth in him.

According to the writer of the holy gospel, there were two thieves crucified along with the Lord Jesus. And the words of the thief are spoken from the cross at the moment of death—surely such an occasion as must guarantee the truth for him of what he says; for who is there that speaks more earnestly than one who is a-dying, when he puts his whole soul into a single utterance! Not that king, satiate with vanities, uttered words of wisdom more deserving of our heed than the deferential utterances of a penitent thief at the moment of death. There were two thieves, but only one has been remembered, the one whom everybody knows when we speak of: The words of the thief on the cross. Which of the thieves it was is indicated neither by naming him nor in any other way, whether he who hung on the right side, or he who hung on the left. And this is not of the slightest consequence, though it may give a childish satisfaction to a curious mind to suppose it was the one on the right; for those on the right are they to whom it shall be said one day: Come, ye blessed of my Father, inherit the kingdom prepared for you from the foundation of the world—and to this thief there was said by the Same who shall say those words, there was said: This very day shalt thou be with me in paradise. The other thief mocked to the end, hardened himself even on the cross—doubtless he hung upon the left.

Luke in his gospel has preserved the words of the thief on the cross:

We receive the due reward of our deeds: but this man hath done nothing amiss. Luke xxiii. 41.

We shall at this time take this text for our consideration, reflecting on

THE JOY IN THE THOUGHT THAT BEFORE GOD A MAN IS ALWAYS ACCOUNTED GUILTY.

Guilty or not guilty?—this is the important question in legal proceedings, and the same question is the yet more important question of our own heart-searching. For though authority can force its way into the darkest corner of the house to apprehend an offender, heart-searching probes still deeper, to find the guilt, than any magistrate can do, into the heart's most secret chamber where God alone is judge.

But as long as it is human judgment with which we are concerned, and as long as it is a situation between one man and another, we are all of one mind that the one thing to be desired is innocence, that innocence is the safe stronghold no injustice or wrong judgment of men can either capture or demolish, that innocence is the purity not even violence can outrage, that it is invulnerable, and death itself can deal it no mortal wound. And yet this is not the exact truth of the matter, and indeed it is true only as long as the situation is essentially a tension between two interests. For in that very relation which is deepest and most tender, in love between one mortal and another, it can be the supreme desire of love to be in the wrong, yea, even to be the guilty one. Humanly speaking, we reckon unhappy love to be the hardest form of suffering, but we may go further, for of unhappy love the hardest, the most agonising, form, is when love's object is essentially unworthy of being loved, and yet it is this object that the lover in his inmost being longs for as for his unique desire. For if love's object is in fact by its nature worthy of being the object, but yet fulfilment is denied, then an unhappy love is less unhappy, less agonising. Then fulfilment may be denied, but the object is not lost; on the contrary, it holds all that perfection in itself that so completely satisfies what love demands. For there is a demand; in all love there is contained a hidden demand, which is not selfish but is eternally and deeply rooted in it, and is itself love's very essence.

We shall suppose such a girl as is unhappy in her love and in her suffering. Might she not speak thus: The question whether I am in the right or in the wrong matters not at all; anyway, I can quite well go on living, for if I am in the wrong he will be ready to forgive me. But if he is in the wrong, if he is guilty, if he is the kind of man who cannot be loved, then it is death to me, then I have lost my all. I have none but this one object of my love, it is he, in the whole world none but he, and alas, he cannot be the object of my love. Nor is the obstacle anything outside himself; if it were, he were still my beloved and I were less unhappy; but in his very soul the obstacle is found—or shall I say, that in the inmost depth of him there is no soul—and I am most unhappy. Therefore she desires the more, rather to be in the wrong herself, even to be the guilty one, if only the beloved may be in the right. What is the meaning of it? It means that this girl truly does love; she does not argue, not even about right and wrong, for then there were two alternatives. Nay, but she truly has become one with her beloved, and therefore she first feels the loss of him when he has lost his essential character—by becoming as one with no character or else essentially a different person! and not when merely by accident he is lost—by becoming another's! If only he might have been in the right, if only she had been the guilty one, then, so she thinks, her love might have been saved; but since he was in the wrong, then, so she thinks, her love is terribly lost to her. And so it is in truth, for nobody is lost to me essentially who is my ideal; if he is lost to another than myself, I can yet love him just as well; but *he* is lost essentially who in the essence of his soul is lost.

But now when a man is confronted with God, and in that situation it is a question of being in the right or in the wrong—is it really possible, I wonder, that anybody ever at any time was capable even of imagining the horror that before God there could be any question of unhappiness in love, for the reason that God was incapable of being its object? Not because God for seventy years leads a man a life, if so it should be, that is harder than any other man's, and so leads him that he understands nothing at all in this dark tally of years, not for this reason is God lost, or lost to him. But if the slightest happening occurred that might prove, or might even assume an appearance of being able to prove, that God was not love, in truth then all were lost, then God were lost. For if God be not love, and if he be not love in everything, then God is not at all. Oh, my hearer, if thou hast known the darkest hour in human life, when all went black before thy soul, as if there were no love in heaven, or as if he who is in heaven after all were aught but love, and when it seemed to thee there was a choice that thou must make, the awful choice between: being in the wrong and gaining God, and being in the right and losing God—oh, then didst thou not find the bliss of heaven in choosing the first? Or, more precisely, in knowing that ultimately it was not a choice, that it was, on the contrary, the eternal demand of heaven upon thee, laid upon thy soul, that there must be no doubt, none, that God was love? Alas, while doubtless there are many who keep the undecided question hidden in their minds, whether in reality God is love, yet it were truly better if they caused the love that is in them to flame up at the mere suggestion of such a horror as that God might not be love, caused love to flame up, for if God is love then also he is love in everything, love in what thou comprehendest, and love in what thou comprehendest not, love in the dark tally that lasts for a day, and in the dark tally that lasts seventy years. Alas, while many call themselves Christians although perhaps they live uncertain whether in reality God is love, it were truly better if they caused the love that is in them to flame up at the mere suggestion of the horrors of paganism: that he who holds the fate of all things and all thy destiny in his hand, that he should be ambiguous, his love no father's fond embrace but a snare set for thee, his hidden being not eternal light but secrecy, and the profoundest depth of his nature not love but a cunning none can comprehend. For indeed it is not required of anybody that he should be able to comprehend the working of God's love, but this is required, that one shall be able to believe, and believing to comprehend, that he is love! It is no terrible thing that thou canst not comprehend the purposes of God, if still he is indeed eternal love, but it is a terrible thing if thou canst not comprehend them because he is unfathomable subterfuge.

But if so it be—as our discourse takes for granted—that a man before God not only is always in the wrong but is always guilty, and therefore also that when he suffers he suffers as a guilty man; then there cannot be any doubt within thee (unless thou wilt sin afresh); and there cannot be any circumstance without thee (unless thou wilt sin afresh by stumbling at it), that is able to do away with the joy in this thought.

The joy is in this, that now, and every moment, and in every moment to come forever, there has happened nothing, and there can happen nothing—should even the most shocking horror conceived by the most morbid imagination come true—nothing that can shake the faith that God is love. And the joy is in this, that if a man will not understand it through what is good, then his very guilt will help him understand. *When a man before God always suffers as a guilty one, then at every moment, no matter what may happen, it is guaranteed that God is love, or, to be more precise, at every moment he is prevented from entering into doubt, by the sense of guilt asserting itself upon him.*

Most people, it is almost certain, have some idea, at times a lively idea, and at moments an intense feeling, that God is love, and yet perhaps there are many who so live as having a vague sense that, if this or that other horror for which they have an especial dread were to come upon them, then they would have to renounce their faith, let go their hold on God, and lose him. But can anything at all be less justifiable than to live thus emptily, to enfeeble the most exalted passion daydreaming between doubt and confidence, so that one never fully faces the treacherous foe that is draining the life-blood from the very heart, so that one never comes to the point of trembling at such a state, but supposes oneself to be not despairing—because one has slept into despair! Oh, it is not God indeed who loses anything by this, but he who sleeps, who verily sins by being asleep, he loses all, he loses that without which life is literally nothing. For as the Scripture speaks[1] of making shipwreck concerning the faith, so it might be said of him who has given up his belief in the love of God that he has suffered shipwreck in respect of the joy of living that pertains to life eternal. What is there more worth living for? If only the ship hold together, let the storm rage; that is something hard to endure. Let good weather come, and a fair wind; that is something cheerful. But if the ship be fatally damaged, what help or hurt does anything else afford? If the planks part, what hope remains? Yet the man who gave up God, who held that any such thing had happened or could happen as to shake belief in the love of God, he verily suffered damage in the close-knit fabric of his inmost being. Whether there is any special name for the ties which hold together the frame of a ship I do not know. But I do know that it is this faith that is the divine compacting in a man, which, holding fast, makes him the proudest craft afloat, but giving way reduces him to a wreck, and thereby makes of the whole substance of his life but triviality and sheer vanity.

Were it at all possible, then, that a man should have even the mere plausibility of justification in abandoning the faith that God is love, he would require first of all to be absolutely pure and altogether free from guilt, not only, as men judge, in this respect or in that, but altogether free from guilt before God. For only on this assumption can there be any foothold for doubt; without it, doubt is not only deprived of a foothold, not only built on sand, but built on an abyss. And after

[1] 1 Tim. i. 19 (R.V.).

that the event must happen which could not be reconciled with the idea that God is love. But such a horror could not be endured by any man. Once only has it been endured—by him who was the Holy One, by him who before God was guiltless. Which is the reason why we ought ever to speak with fear and trembling and an inclination to the quietness of worship about Christ's passion. For human thought no more than human language can imagine or conceive with clearness anything so terrible. That is why one should speak with the restraint of humility or in humility keep silent, about how Christ suffered, lest one be led into temptation through an impious thirst for probing into the secrets of God, the penalty of which was represented, even in paganism, as a parching thirst forever. That is why one should have a care, especially in these days, when in so many ways we want to worry the life out of faith, as if to believe were to understand, as if nobody could venture to believe, and believe unto salvation, who did not arrogantly claim to understand. Only Christ *before God* was guiltless, and for that very reason did he have to endure a superhuman suffering, to be led, as it were, to the limit of despondency, to the question whether God indeed was love, when he cried: My God, my God, why hast thou forsaken me? But it was not so with the thief of whom we are speaking. And therefore, while the Saviour of the world is moaning: My God, my God, why hast thou forsaken me?—words which he who was both our Church's greatest preacher and also its strictest Christian believer, words which Luther, just because of his strict Christian faith, would hardly dare to preach upon —at the same time the thief is preaching by the Saviour's side, as becomes a preacher, first and foremost to his own edification, on this for the subject of his pious contemplation: It is as a guilty man that I suffer.

Whereas the passion of Christ in the depth of its horror cannot be the subject matter of preaching, the theme of the thief is a theme most proper to be preached. For truly under the name of preaching we hear many an insipid, many a sickening utterance about the love of God; but this penitential discourse, on sin and guilt, is the only veritably fitting introduction of which the love of God must be the conclusion. It is the penitent thief who truly preaches; if the king is called the Preacher, how much more truly the penitential thief is one. He is the one who is fit to preach repentance; for a coat of camel's hair is certainly a constricting garment, but crucifixion is a position more constricting still; and it is certainly a poor position in life that one should dwell in the wilderness, but crucifixion is quite the hardest position to occupy; and to say Repent ye! is not quite so excellent a sermon on repentance as to say: It is as a guilty man that *I* am suffering; and to say of oneself: I am a Prophet not quite so stirring as to say: I am a sinner and it is as a guilty man that I suffer. The thief is preaching to himself, and to the other thief, and to all that are present there, and he says: All of you are sinners; only he who hangs between us, only he is without guilt before God, and suffers in his innocence. For, says this uplifted preacher of repentance, it is otherwise in the world, and men commonly put one thief between two upright men, but the propriety of this is but a fiction. Here is displayed the truth: he who is the only Righteous One, the only One, is crucified between two thieves. Lo, therefore do the scriptures say: "He was numbered with the transgressors"—but not because we two are thieves, and so as men reckon it, are sinners beyond all other men. Nay, but take me down, and, of all the people here, hang up in place of me whomsoever you will, and he, the Holy One, as being crucified along with such a person, is numbered with transgressors. Yea, whenever he, the Holy One, is numbered with the human race, he is numbered with transgressors. Or can it be, I wonder, that there is anybody—yea, even one who in a human sense is innocently accused, is innocently convicted, is innocently crucified—who, alongside him who is here crucified, would dare to say: In innocence I suffer! This is a Christian call to repentance, reminding even the martyr that before God he suffers as a guilty man.

It is a Christian call to repentance, for the Jewish mind rests on the conception that there are holy men who are to preach repentance, and that a man by his own effort can become so holy as to be a preacher of repentance. In Christianity, on the contrary, it is a veritable sinner who preaches repentance, and even such as in a human sense are holy men must bow before the fact that a veritable sinner is the preacher of repentance, one who does not say: Woe unto you! when he begins, but says instead: May God be merciful to me, a sinner; it is as a guilty man that I suffer.

Yet the penitent thief is no preacher of repentance, his preaching is not a call to repent; if it were, then it would have nothing to do with the theme of the present discourse; the joy that is in the thought that before God a man always suffers as one who is guilty. But it is just on this theme that the thief is preaching, for his own assurance and comfort. This is what edifies and instructs us in this thief, that in the hour of a most shameful death he has enough depth and humility to find it a comfort to suffer as a guilty man, and that too, over against the agony of a death suffered on the cross that stands between. The penitent thief finds comfort and assurance, over against that suffering, in the thought that he is suffering as a guilty man, and wherefore, but that then his suffering does not broach the question, the anxious question asked in the fearfulness of doubt, whether God is love. And thus the thief is not a preacher of repentance, except as the glad message of the Gospel is; he declares the joy that is painful only in the humiliation of the proud.

In the pagan world, when a man suffered injustice at the hands of other men, was persecuted for righteousness' sake, was condemned to lose his life for righteousness' sake, then, ah then, he also became convinced of his own importance, and *before God* he averred: In innocence I suffer—and proudly thought that that was best—that he should be in the right! But alongside Christ such a man learns that in the sight of God there is but one who has suffered in innocence, and this makes him humble. In paganism, because a man in relation to men was in one point right—or is that not enough? then let us say because in relation to men he was in all points right —he would transfer this to his relation to God, and be in one point right in the sight of God—before whom man is in truth in all points wrong! The pagan was so proud and so deluded that he failed to realise how terrible this was, and congratulated himself upon his "splendid sin"[1] as if upon virtue.

And so the thief finds comfort in the thought that he suffers as a guilty man. And this too is over against the fearful thought that one might suffer when before God one is guiltless. For when one suffers as a guilty man and makes confession of it, then one has God to hope in, God to hold to, then one has— if I may dare say so—kept God!—and what peril could not a man endure; yea, even in his consuming wrath to have him still—siding with one! But when one suffers as in the sight of God quite innocent, then it is as if one had God against one, then one is—God-forsaken! When one suffers as a guilty man, then the distress humiliates, and yet in it is the consolation of eternity, the very joy of eternity: to let God be righteous; but when one suffers altogether innocently, then it seems to be not quite clear that God is love, and then it seems as if the issue had to do with vindicating God, which only the imagination of fools and the vain imagination of philosophy can consider as the easiest way—for man it is in truth presumption.

For what would doubt of God's love aim at doing? It would reverse the relation, and would sit secure at ease, to judge, considering whether God was truly love. It would make God the defendant, make him the one on whom to lay demand. But never in this way shall the love of God be found, accursed of God shall be doubt's searching after God, since as presumption it sets out. On the other hand, it is the blessedness of faith, that God is love. From this it does not follow that faith understands how the working out of the will of God for a man is love. And this is just faith's conflict: to believe without

[1] Augustine's description of pagan virtue.

being able to understand. And so when this conflict of faith begins, when doubts would rise up, or when "Doubt with its wild thoughts rages against the faith",[1] then the sense of sin breaks in, a relieving force, a final reinforcement. It might be supposed to be a hostile power, but no, it is to help our faith it comes, to help a believer by teaching him, not to doubt God, but to doubt himself. Instead of the delusive expedient of thinking out one's faith, which is just the most dangerous expedient that doubt can employ, the sense of sin will thunder, Halt!—and bring back rescued faith, thus rescued in that no doubt was left, whether God were love. For as the Scripture says that God has concluded all under sin that every mouth may be stopped,[2] so this thought, which not only humbles but saves, stops the mouth of our doubts. When doubts would assail faith, asking a thousand questions, and make it seem as if God could not answer, then the believer is taught by his sense of sin that it is he who for a thousand questions cannot produce one answer. Ergo, God is love. Is the perfect efficacy of such an inference beyond thy comprehension? yet faith can comprehend it. Is the joy beyond thy comprehension that thus forever it is confirmed that God is love? Yet faith can comprehend. It understands that, while it is a fantasy to dream of being able to think out faith, it is blessedness to find it impossible to doubt. Does it appal us that a son should be in the right as against his father? Does the thought edify us that a son is in the wrong—*always*—as against his father? Oh, then is this truly blessed, that we find ourselves unable to doubt whether God be love. Let the mere empty praise of the love of God be silenced, for its true vindication is in this, that as a guilty man I suffer always—so sure to all eternity it is that God is love. In paganism this most blessed of all thoughts had no better assurance, alas, but that a man might opine himself to be in the right over against God: in Christianity it is perpetually assured. And now if this be the only joyful thought in both heaven and earth, if "Rejoice, and again I say

---

[1] Quotation from a hymn by Brorson. [2] Gal. iii. 22 and Rom. iii. 19.

rejoice" spring only from the truth that God is love, then it is joy indeed that the truth is so firmly established that no doubt, none, can move it, nor come near moving it. For the sense of sin is the mighty guardian of this precious thing. Doubt, when it would attack, is that very moment doomed: then that great power thrusts it into the abyss, down to the nothingness from whence it came; and in that moment faith has once more its object, namely, that God is love. So here can be no talk, misleading talk, of a doubtful victory—or, to be more correct, of the sure victory of doubt—but here we speak with assurance of the certain death of doubt, of its certain death at birth! If doubt is to have the merest pretence of a foundation, it must be able to plead innocence not in comparison with other men, and not in this or that particular, but innocence *before God.* And if it have not such an innocence, as it cannot have, then it is the same moment utterly destroyed, reduced to nothing; reduced to nothing!—Oh, this is just the opposite of setting out from nothing.

Since it is the presupposition of our discourse that a man before God is always guilty, this is *the joy in it: that the fault is therefore with the man, and consequently there must be always something to be done, there must be tasks, that are moreover human tasks,* and with the tasks a hope, that everything can and will be better, when he becomes better, more diligent, more prayerful, more obedient, more humble, more devout, more ardent in his love, more fervent in spirit.

Is this not matter for rejoicing? For if it be that courage says, and truly says: Where danger is, there too am I; or turns it about and says: Where I am, there is danger; and if it be that loving sympathy can say, and truly say: Yet harder than the sufferer's lot it is to sit beside him having naught to do; then must it be that where there is a task there too there is a hope. But if a man before God is always guilty, then it follows that there is always a task and always a hope. O my hearer, if thou hast been tried in life, if thou hast been so far tried that one can speak with thee of what is terrible, because thou hast been acquainted with other dangers and with other terrors than those that pettiness and cowardice and slackness, like a naughty child, are accustomed to whimper over, as, that one does not get one's own way at once, that one has to put up with something, that one does not meet with success at once, that God takes no notice of one's indignation—if thou hast been more greatly tried, then is not this the truth, that here thou didst realise thou hadst come to the moment of the hardest suffering, in the pause in which it seemed there was no task to perform? Here was no sufferer loth to lift a burden because it was so heavy: it was what is heavier still, that there seemed to be no task to perform, and the very suffering could not be the task. Here was no sufferer who, after labouring long in vain, was now a rebel against God and would labour no longer; alas, no, it was something unspeakably heavier to bear: that his labour did not seem to him to be required by any task given him to perform. Here was no sufferer who having so many times snatched at a false prize had now grown tired of beginning at the beginning; nay, rather it was the horror of hopelessness, as if there were no point at which to begin, as if with the best of wills he could find no task to perform. For when we see the horse, already, it may be, in distress, on which too great a burden has been laid, when we see it make a last attempt, strain every sinew to drag on its load, then we give it sympathy, but also have the hope that it may still succeed. But didst thou see a horse in cruel agony and straining every sinew, and yet didst see no task, no load, would it not be that this were a sight to evoke despair? And is it truly hopelessness to give up one's task because it is so hard, or is it truly hopelessness almost to faint beneath one's burden because it is so heavy, or is it truly hopelessness to give up hope from very fear of one's task? Ah no, but this is hopelessness: that one should exert all the power of one's will—and have no task to perform! Didst ever thou see a man in peril on the sea, would it not be that thou wouldst fear for him, wouldst behold with a shudder of sympathy—and yet wouldst hope! But didst thou see, again, one who from heedlessness was sinking in a bog, would it not be that this were a sight to evoke despair? Wouldst thou not behold with the chill of horror? For what was lacking was not strength, and what was lacking was not the will to use his strength, but what was lacking was—the task! Whether the strength of such an unfortunate be much or little and whether he uses it or not, in any case he sinks, not under the heavy weight of his task, and not beneath its greatness, but he sinks in that treacherous illusion, that there is no task for him to do.

Yea, when there is nothing to be done, and when even suffering itself presents no task, then there is hopelessness, and then there is a grim freedom from labour, freedom to perish slowly in hopelessness. So long as there is a task to perform, so long as there is an allotted task, so long is a man not abandoned without hope; so long as there is a task to perform, so long is there a way of shortening the time, for labour and effort shorten the time. But when there is nothing to be done, when there is no task, but only the mockery of that deep treachery that denies there is a task, then there is hopelessness, and then there is a deadly endlessness of time.

Therefore only if there be nothing to be done, and if he who says so be without guilt *before God*—for when he is guilty then there is always certainly something to be done—only if there be nothing to be done, which is to be understood as if there were nothing required, only then is there hopelessness. Because when it is said that there is nothing to be done, it does not by any means follow that there is no task required, for patience can be the task. But if there be no task, and if the sufferer be without guilt before God, then and then only is there no hope. And so if a sufferer could be in the right, confronting God, if it were possible that the fault could be with God, why then, there would be hopelessness, and the horror of hopelessness, which is that there would be no task to perform. For the tasks of faith and hope, as well as of love and patience and humility and obedience, in short, all human tasks, abide in the eternal truth, wherein they have their home and reason for their being. Had it ever happened to a man as before God that the fault lay with God, then there were no task to perform; had this ever happened to any man then for all mankind there had been no tasks to perform. It never was, in any single instance, that there was no task to perform; nay, but if God just once had shown that he was not love, in the least thing or the greatest, had left a sufferer with no task to perform, then for all men no longer were there any task; then were it but trumpery gain, and empty glory, and the sore affliction of vexation of spirit, to believe; and self-contradiction to labour; and a bitter anguish to live. Out of the heart are the issues of life, and if a man receive injury there, then he himself is to blame if there is nothing left for him but the restless, galling toil of sin and vanity. But from the heart of God issues the life that is in all things, the life that consists in doing the tasks he gives us to do. If it be true that a creature must die when God causes his spirit to return to him, then it is true also that if God should but for an instant have denied his love, then all our tasks are dead, reduced to nothing, and only hopelessness remains.

Ah, yes, most feel no doubt at times, and confess it to themselves, that in this or that other matter they were themselves to blame; and yet, it may be secretly, in many a heart the dark thought still abides, that it could happen, and perhaps had happened, and God after all was to blame, for this—that a man was lost! And so we live our lives away, preoccupied and busy with all else that concerns us; we do not think of ourselves as being in despair, nor come to shudder at that situation, because no light has been allowed to penetrate the gloom. Dimly, indeed, we did not even wish it should, for that inward dimness is uneasily aware, how embarrassing a clearness it would be to understand the demand God makes on a human soul, how embarrassing a clearness to understand that always there is a task for us to do. But is only that man mortal who is dead? Is it not rather the living man whose certain fate is death who is called and who is a mortal? And so is not he too in a situation of despair, who never came to the point of despairing, because he did not even realise that he was in despair! Or when a merchant making up his accounts finds he is ruined—and is desperate, is he any more in despair than the merchant who dimly knows that things are wrong, but hopes to escape his liabilities for some time longer? Is it to be more in despair, when one despairs about the truth, than not to dare to come to the truth? And every man in whose heart this dark thought about God is dwelling is a despairing man; it can be seen in the demeanour of his spirit, for before God he is not like him who casts down his eyes in consciousness of his guilt, his moral debt to God, nor yet like him who, humbly but with confidence, lifts up his face to God. Nay, but he skulks in the shadow.

Yet it were truly better than skulking, were the darkness dissipated, and one came to shudder at the horror, a horror that belongs in fact to paganism, of a God unable, or unwilling, to give a man confidence and courage. For no false god can either make a man as nothing—make him feel the nonentity he is—since for that the false god is too feeble; neither can a false god give a man confidence—since for that he is not strong enough. Therefore we may say it was the false god who taught the pagan to skulk in shadows. The very wisest of pagans who ever lived, even he, however much wiser he was in other respects than the humblest of believers, compared with him has a darkness within his soul; because in the last analysis it could not for the pagan be eternally clear and certain, whether the fault was with himself, or whether that rare case might not be, when the fault was with his god; whether hopelessness were not after all a state in which a man may find himself when he is guiltless, because it is the god who is at fault in leaving the man without a task to do. Hence we can only excuse the pagan, because his god himself is darkness.

But the God of the Christian is light, and therefore every man is without excuse and inexcusable. But if thou take away all excuses, yea, take away the fertile dark indolence that spawns excuses, then is there no darkness; and if thou take away all excuses, then a man is without excuse, and always without excuse; but if never before God is he pure and is always without excuse; then he is always guilty, even when he suffers. But if always he suffers as a guilty man, then it is eternally certain that God is love, and so it is a joy that there are always tasks, there is always something to be done.

Ought not this to make us glad? What! somebody says, That a man before God suffers always as guilty? Yea, when this is rightly understood to mean that it is eternally certain that God is love, and that there is always some task he requires of us. See how doubt, with absolute complacency and shameless presumption, would force its way into the very being of God, to prove that God is love. But never to all eternity shall it succeed in proving it, starting from presumption. And what, after all, is doubt indeed, what else but that very same dim gloom, what else but the source of all our excuses, and *the excuse* which would reverse our relation to him—and would doubt God! But if so it be, and if so it ought to be, that a man must doubt God's love, then the man has his excuse. If, on the contrary, to doubt the love of God is to presume, then the man has no excuse, he is the one who is accused, and he is guilty, and ever committed in duty to some task. This is the rule in the matter, but it is also a joyful thing that so there is always a task. If the starting-point be doubt, then long, long before the end God is lost to us, and a man is exempt, not only from having forever a task to perform, but also from having forever the comfort of a task forever awaiting him. If, on the other hand, a sense of sin be the starting-point, then the starting of doubt is made impossible, and so there is the joy, that there always is a task.

The joy in it then is this, that it is forever sure that God is love, and more precisely the joy is in always having a task committed to us. While there is life there is hope. But while there is a task there is life, and while there is life there is hope, and the task itself is not only a hope of further life, but a present joy. One who has faith therefore, remembering that before God a man is always accounted guilty, will dare to say: Whatever happens to me, there is something to do, and always, in all circumstances, I have a task to perform; hopelessness is a horror that can find no place if a man be not so presumptuous as to abandon himself. Yea, even should the heaviest lot be mine, such as none ever had before, and though there were nothing to be done, not anything at all, yet there is this of joy—that a task is committed to me, for then the task is to bear my lot with patience. And should the uttermost patience be required of me, such as was never required of any man before, yet there is this of joy—that the task is committed to me not to lose hold on patience, even to the very end. By means of the sense of sin it becomes impossible to doubt that God is love: in consequence it is forever sure that God is love. But if this is forever sure then there are always tasks to perform, for all tasks have their ground in God. And if a man before God is always accounted guilty, then there is always a task to perform. And this is how it comes about that always having a task to perform and the abiding certainty that God is love are one and the same thing, and that they both are comprehended in the truth that a man is always guilty in relation to God.

Let us remind ourselves of the penitent thief. Can we say of him that he proclaims the consolation to be found in being judged guilty, the consolation that there always is a task to perform? It might seem as if the thief lacked opportunity; one who is crucified has not many moments left, he has his additional reason for supposing that he cannot speak any more of tasks to perform.

And yet it is not so. In comparison with the more than human suffering borne by that other Crucified One, the thief finds consolation and relief in the thought that he is suffering for guilt, and therefore also finds that there remains a task for him, the last—but is it not verily his last hour! Just because he is suffering as a guilty man he finds here some consolation and relief from suffering, in that he has a task, and that task is—repentance and remorse! And while the Saviour of the world is sighing: My God, my God, why hast thou forsaken me!—the penitent thief is humiliated by the knowledge—and yet it is some relief of his suffering too—that it is not God who has forsaken him, but he who has forsaken God. And, penitent, he says to the One who is crucified along with him: Remember me, when thou comest into thy kingdom. Heavy is that suffering of a mortal man, who in the agony of death, facing death's terror, with late repentance reaches out to the mercy of God, but even in this the penitent thief finds some relief of suffering, when he compares his own with the superhuman suffering that it is to be forsaken of God. For to be forsaken of God—ah, that is indeed to be without a task, that is the ultimate deprivation of what each man always has, the task of patience, grounded in the truth that God has not forsaken the sufferer. And therefore is the passion of Christ beyond human suffering, and his patience more than human, so that no mortal may comprehend either the one or the other of these. And though it may be well that we should speak in merely human terms of the suffering of Christ—if in such a way only we should speak of him, as that he of all men suffered most, we are blaspheming against God; for though his suffering be human, yet it is superhuman too, and there yawns forever an abyss set deep between his suffering and that of man.

Perhaps another thought as well was stirring in the soul of that penitent thief. Perhaps he said to himself: If there should come this very instant an order from the governor, to take down those who have been crucified and let them live, then I, who have suffered for my guilt, should have this comfort, that there are plenty of tasks awaiting me. But as for him who is the Holy One, the Innocent One, there is no task for him; he has had a more than human task. He has *in the sight of God* nothing with which to reproach himself, nothing; his life has been obedience, and yet he has been forsaken by God! Lo, this is the more than human suffering, says the penitent thief;

no man has suffered thus, no man can ever suffer thus, for as no man is guiltless *in the sight of God*, so neither can any ever have been, nor ever be said to be about to be forsaken by God. But it is in his guilt that a man knows suffering, and God has not forsaken him, for there ever remains the task, and where the task is there is hope, and in having a task to perform and a hope to cherish he finds his comfort. Such comfort is for everyone who confesses that he suffers for his guilt; it is even for me, who am lost, a crucified thief; it is true for me there is nothing now to do—ah, even now the pangs of death are on me!—but yet there is for me a task, and I am not forsaken of God. And this, moreover, is no dreary utterance of woe, except for one who is defiant, who refuses to look on what is terrible, and for whom true joy is an offence; but anyone who humbles himself, anyone who is of the truth sufficiently to know the terrible, knows also what the thief proclaims is joy.

Is it so, however, in very truth, that before God a man suffers always as one found guilty? Or could it be that the intention of this discourse is to raise up contradictory thoughts, and to confuse our notions, to talk out of existence the comfort he has who is accounted by men an innocent sufferer, the comfort that he is suffering in innocence, and to talk false comfort for him who is accounted by men to suffer for his guilt, inasmuch as in our sense it is for guilt that everyone is suffering all the time?

Not so. There is only one intention in our discourse, and that I dare call the highest, there is only one thing it seeks, and that I dare call the highest: by every manner of means to make it forever sure that God is love. In truth, to seek this end is beyond any doubt to bend all our thinking to the highest! For by whatever means we establish the certainty of it, even if the means at first glance seem to be hard and painful; so as the end be won indeed, in an added assurance that God is love, then this is what is joyous. The thought that God is love holds within itself all joy, that every means by which this thought may gain in clearness and assurance, every means, even the most painful, is joyous. In the thought that God is love is held the whole blessed persuasiveness of the eternal: the way therefore, even should it be the most painful of ways, and the conditions laid down, even should they be the bitterest, consist in absolute joy. And so, should it not be as here we have assumed, that a man in the sight of God suffers ever as one who is guilty, while yet it is true as here we have propounded it, that joy is in this thought; then a man must wish that what we have assumed were true indeed; one who is of the truth must say: Since this is clear to me, that, if in the sight of God I suffer ever as a guilty man, it is eternal truth that God is love, then I shall but desire that it may be ever clear to me, and ever in my thought, that as a guilty man I suffer.

And yet if we are not to require of a man that he should desire this (although for a proper understanding of it, it must be so near his heart that he does desire it, for if so be that his inclination urges on his effort then he has that understanding which only eagerness of desire helps over difficulties); still it is true as pure matter of fact that a man in the sight of God suffers ever as one who is guilty—and eternally certain that God is love! Let others then show only the satisfaction they derive from thinking out their faith. This is beyond my powers, and that kind of satisfaction is not to my mind; I find joy and assurance of joy through the edifying consideration that one can make it impossible to begin to doubt, and that the consciousness of sin safeguards the joy.

And now we shall consider more precisely what this discourse presupposed. We shall not allow ourselves to be disturbed by the fact that it was a thief who spoke the words that were read out, and that he spoke them about himself, for even a thief can with these very words have said what matters greatly. But neither shall we try to conceal how it is true especially of the thief that he suffers as a guilty man. For we make a just distinction between what it is to be a wrongdoer and what it is to suffer as a guilty man, since it does not follow from his being a wrongdoer that he suffers as a guilty man. Consequently, there are three definitions over which our discourse must linger: when a man by men is accounted guilty, then he suffers as a guilty man in relation to God and to men; when a man by men is accounted guiltless, then we men say of him with reference to God that over against God he is in the wrong; and: before God a man always suffers as one who is guilty.

When a man, in a human sense, is guilty, then he suffers as a guilty man in relation both to God and to men. This is the case of the thief—he is a criminal who bears his punishment. The true thing in him is, that he himself makes full, profound admission that he suffers as a guilty man. Even in such cases, alas, there is sometimes heard from one who is guilty, blasphemous talk that would repudiate the guilt, shameless and presumptuous talk, that the evil tendency was born with him, that his crime was caused by neglect in his upbringing, and so on.

This was the first case. The second is when a man in a human sense suffers without guilt, but we men say of him with reference to God that over against God he is in the wrong. So it is not the sufferer who is speaking to himself about his relation to God, but we others who, in the third person, are speaking of that sufferer's relation to God. The case is described specifically when we say God tries a man. To name one of the shining examples of men who were tried and stood the test, take Job. Who indeed would think of saying that Job in human judgment suffered as one who was guilty! Were such a way of speaking not blasphemy, yet it were presumption towards a proper object of our veneration—Job, who shall be as he has been and as he is, a pattern for the race. Who of the human race would dare to speak so of him! Even God in heaven speaks, we might say, with something of partiality, so humanly indeed that it is as if he were proud of Job, saying to

Satan: "Hast thou considered my servant Job?" So does a man speak of anything he has which gives him pride; so does a man speak of one of whom he feels so confident that he ventures to challenge him with danger for the bare sake of the joy of seeing him triumphant.

And so, from a human point of view Job suffers as one who is free from guilt; he has neither fault nor crime with which to reproach himself, but on the contrary his life and conduct have been as in the sight of God, and winning praise from men; for it is not on the day of his affliction that Job first becomes the pattern, so was he in the good days as well, and therefore was he well prepared to stand fast in his trial. But Job is none the less forever in the wrong towards God. God's thoughts eternally are higher than the thoughts of man, from which it follows that every conception a man has of happiness and of unhappiness, of what is joyful and of what is sad, is a wrong thought. As a man continues in this sphere of concepts he constantly retains his condition of being in the wrong towards God, and he emerges from this sphere of concepts only by acknowledging that towards God he is forever in the wrong.

But now, when impatience begins to stir in the sufferer by men reckoned guiltless, in him whom God is trying, and when, because in a human view he is in the right, because he is in the right about this or that, he would fain by any means be in the right towards God, what then? Is he to be permitted, or is he able, to reverse the relation and be in the right towards God (for this is to reverse the relation; as a man is forever in the wrong towards God, so everything would be reversed if but once, in the merest trifle, he were in the right); is the doubter to maintain his position of being in the right, in other words, is everything to be lost? Nay, for then something else takes place, then in his trial the man understands that instead of speaking with other men he must speak with himself before God; and we others, in our respect for him who is tried, understand that there is no more we dare say, that we dare not make him guilty. And so in his trial he speaks with himself before God, and then into the conflict comes the ultimate reinforcement: that in relation to God it is forever as a guilty man that a man must suffer.

Fundamentally, the relation between God and man is in this, that a man is a sinner, and God is the Holy One. Confronting God a man is not a sinner in this or that regard, but in his being he is sinful, not guilty in this or that, but guilty essentially and absolutely. But if he is essentially guilty then also he is always guilty, because the indebtedness of essential guilt is so profound as to make impossible every superficial distinction. Between man and man the relation is in this, that a man may be in the right in one matter and wrong in another, be guiltless in this and be guilty in that; but such a relation between God and a man cannot be, for, if it were, then God were not God but the equal of man, and if it were, then the guilt were not of any essential importance.

And yet in ordinary daily life a man is not every moment conscious of the fundamental relation, for no mortal could endure it; in ordinary daily life a man lives more or less within a scheme where all is determined by human standards, whereas the relation that is fundamental must of course determine what he is with reference to God. The fundamental relation however is not lacking; on the contrary, it is deeper than anything else in the man's soul. Just so in the state the law is always in existence, but is as it were dormant; as soon, however, as a crime is committed, the law bestirs itself, and then, as it were, steps out of its quiescence and asserts its authority;[1] so is it with the fundamental relation of a man to God. When confusion would break in, and impatience stare itself giddy on its one idea, and in the end turn all things upside down, then the fundamental relation asserts itself. When, so to speak, impatience would rise in revolt against God and would contend with God as a man contends against his equal, protesting

---

[1] cf. *Measure for Measure*, Act II, Scene 2: "The law hath not been dead though it hath slept."

he is in the right, then there is something else that happens, for the fundamental relation rises in revolt against the impatient man, and teaches him that before God a man is in his very nature guilty, and therefore *always* guilty. The guilt in which a man finds himself before God lies not in this or that, the relation between them is not in that way to be adjusted, his is an eternal guilt, and therefore is he always guilty; at any moment he may choose, God can affirm the fundamental guilt, and even if a man should be, in a human way of speaking, right in everything, he is none the less, in relation to God, always guilty. Even the mightiest of kings, when he opposes the most unquestionable superiority to an insurgent, fights by the means of the strong effective forces on his side; but God in heaven fights by transferring the attack to the side of the aggressor—and when, so to speak, impatience like a rebel would assail God, the consciousness of sin attacks the rebel, that is, the aggressor finds that he is fighting with himself. The omnipotence and holiness of God do not mean that he can triumph over all mankind, as being the stronger, for this would be to make a direct comparison; but they do mean, what excludes all comparison, that nobody can attain to fighting against him.

This was the third definition and the subject of our discourse: that a man before God suffers always as one who is guilty. Or ought the point of our discourse to be, that a man, whenever he suffers, must torture himself by imagining his suffering a punishment for this or that specific offence? By no means. One who in a human sense suffers in innocence, even he shall humbly believe himself to be before God in the wrong. But if in this he does not succeed, but is doubtful and impatient, then shall the final thought, the real examiner, instruct him that his suffering is not merely a punishment for this or for that precise offence (for if it were so, then therefore it would follow that in something he well might be in the right), but that his guilt is an eternal guilt, and hence he is always guilty. But what is not true is just that we, being afraid, would fain put undeserved suffering alongside punishment for this or that particular offence, as if apart from that a man were not quite guilty, as if God were a cruel monster, prosecuting some particular offence, as if a man were not always guilty.

See how this was what the friends of Job no doubt really wanted to say to Job: that a man before God suffers always as one who is guilty. Nor indeed was this untrue; their error was different, that they should want to take upon themselves, or to arrogate to themselves the right, to say this to him, for none has such a right in relation to another. And, neither did Job's friends have any standard to measure what this might mean: *before God* to suffer *in innocence*. The highest thing known to the Jews was just such a piety as Job's; and therefore it was doubly arrogant and doubly unjust in his friends to speak in such terms to Job. The Christian knows, on the other hand, that there is only One, but knows too that there is One, who before God has suffered in innocence. With him none dare compare himself, or apply his measure to himself; between him and every man is an eternal difference: whence it is manifest now with fresh clearness, that before God a man suffers always as one who is guilty.

So what we assumed stands firm. Moreover this too stands firm, developed from our assumption, it stands firm that there is joy in the fact that a man before God suffers always as one who is guilty. But it is a joy that humbles. While it holds good that nobody has any right to say it by way of passing judgment on such another as men would call an innocent sufferer, yet the man who is tried must know that if he will but put it to the test he shall prove for himself the joy that lies in this thought. For if a mind in suspense is always at strain, and if it is dreary to be unable to reach a conclusion—this thought, indeed is a conclusive one! If any sought to think his doubt away, then it might happen that, just when he supposed he had done it, he found there was one doubt he had forgotten, and so must begin all over again; but this abiding and concluding thought is a genuine conclusion just because it is the same at the beginning as at the end; this thought is a conclusion, yea, the only one with which we truly can begin, and it is moreover the only conclusion with which we can end. But also it has invincible strength. It is not like a knight errant who goes out to encounter adventure in his life, while still it is doubtful what may befall him and what *will become* of him, nay, but it is one throughly furnished in warrior's panoply, lacking nothing, and already it is *what it will become*. For it is a man's will, and yet this does not fully express it, but it is a man's will in covenant with God, and it is a man's will resolved before God, resolved in awareness of dangers, but resolved as well in a covenant with victory.

V

It is a commonly-accepted figure of speech, used by everybody, to compare life with a way; and indeed there are many fruitful applications of the parallel; but not less worth considering is the unavoidable difference. In a material sense the way is an objective reality, and it does not matter whether anybody walks on it or not, nor does it matter how each traveller fares, for the way is still the way. But in a spiritual sense the way cannot of course be indicated to physical sight; no doubt there is a sense in which it exists whether anybody goes on it or not, and yet, in another sense, for each person the way first exists, or comes into existence, when he goes on it, for the way is *the manner* of our going. We cannot point to the path of virtue, and say: "There lies the path of virtue"; we can only speak of how one treads the path of virtue; and when anybody will not go just like that, then he is going by another way. It would not, on the other hand, be a rational mode of speech, if we were to define a highway by *the manner* of men's treading it. Whether it be a youth who, undaunted in spirit and head erect, goes with light springing step, or a man enfeebled by years, who, head bent, is slowly toiling onward; whether it be a favourite of fortune who is hurrying forward to the goal of his desire, or an anxious soul who, having turned away from his desire, is labouring heavily on; whether it be a poor homeless wanderer or a rich man in his splendid coach, the way is alike for all, the way is and abides the same, the same highway.

The limitations of the analogy in the figure appear most clearly when we speak of a way at one and the same time in the material and the spiritual sense. Thus, when we read what the Holy Gospel says of the Good Samaritan, it speaks of the way between Jericho and Jerusalem, and we are told of at least three, perhaps even five, people, that they "came down that way"; whereas, speaking in a spiritual sense, we must say that in fact each went his own way—ah, the highway marks no difference between them; it is the spirit that makes that difference, and the difference between the ways they take. The first of them was a peaceful traveller, taking the way from Jericho to Jerusalem,[1] perhaps on business, perhaps for a religious purpose, but anyhow travelling peacefully upon his lawful occasions. The second was a robber, who went "that way", and yet it was the way of lawlessness. Then "that way" came a priest; he saw the unfortunate who had been mauled by the robber, and perhaps for an instant had some compunction about him, but none the less went on, by the way of the shallow mind, that is quickly but not deeply moved. Afterwards "by that way" came a Levite; he saw the unfortunate and went by unmoved, continuing his way—ah, the highway did not belong to any of the travellers, and yet the Levite went on "that way" by his own way, the way of selfishness and a hard heart. Finally, "that way" came a Samaritan; he found the victim on the way of compassion; he showed by his example how to go on the way of compassion, showed that, in a spiritual sense, the way is the same thing as how one goes on it.

And so the Gospel says to the reader: "Go, and do thou likewise", which is to say: When thou dost take thy way as the Samaritan did, then thou art on the way of compassion; for the road between Jericho and Jerusalem has no monopoly of acts of compassion. It all happened on "that way", and yet in the first case it was the way of peace, in the second, the way of lawlessness, in the third the way of shallowness, in the fourth the way of hard-heartedness, and in the fifth the way of compassion. There were five travellers who, says the Gospel, went "that way"; yet each went his own way.

So then in a matter of the spirit; it is how one goes upon life's way that marks the difference of the different ways. For

---

[1] Luke x. 30. This should of course be "from Jerusalem to Jericho" (trans.).

in so far as life, or, quite simply, the general notion of what it is to be alive, is compared with a way, then the figure expresses only the universal concept, what all living creatures have in common in being alive, inasmuch as they all go by the same way; all are on life's way. But when we come down to considering seriously what life means, then it is a question of how one ought to go, in order that on life's way one may go by the right way; this is the question for the wayfarer, not, as he might have asked it: Where does this way lead?—but: How does one go on this way, and, how ought one to go?

For some serious consideration is called for if anybody is going to ask the right question. Because impatience is prone to be deceived, and would ask, in the spiritual sense also, only where the way may be, as if that settled everything, as it does when the wayfarer comes upon the highway. And worldly wisdom is very ready to deceive, answering again and again the question where the way may be, and ignoring the difficulty that in any spiritual sense the way is *the manner* of our going. Sometimes worldly wisdom would teach that the way goes by Gerezim, and sometimes by Moriah;[1] sometimes that it goes by one or other of the sciences, sometimes that it is in certain dogmas, sometimes in a certain external mode of conduct; nor will a man acknowledge to himself that this is all deception, inasmuch as the way is—how he goes! For it is even as the Scriptures say,[2] that there can be two men sleeping in the same bed, and the one is saved, the other lost; two men can go up to the same House of God, and the one goes home saved, the other lost;[3] two men can repeat the whole of the same confession of faith, and the one is saved, the other lost. Whence does this arise but from the verity that it is illusion to know the way in a spiritual sense by where it goes, inasmuch as it is—how we go!

But even he who has learned to ask the right question, how he ought to go? asks about one thing further, namely,

[1] John iv. 21. [2] Luke xvii. 34. [3] Luke xviii. 10.

whither does it lead? All glorifying of the perfection of the way can really not mean anything if the way does not lead to perfection—ah, the more perfect the way, if it led but to destruction, the more sorrowful would it be; and, on the other hand, no matter how painful and how laborious the going, so long as it really is the way of perfection, it is still a joyful way.

How then does one go by the way of perfection? For by the way of pleasure one goes as lightly as in a dance; by the way of honour one walks proudly, with a garland crowned; by the easy way of happiness one goes with every desire gratified. But how does one go by the way of perfection? He who asks in earnest, who, standing on the way, asks about the old paths, shall in very earnest receive an answer, even the ancient answer: that the way is strait and narrow, and that a man goes on the way of perfection in straitened circumstances. And whether thou dost enquire of the scriptures of the Old Testament or of the New, on this there is only one finding; there are many answers but they all say the same thing; the answer is always the same and only the voice is different, so that through such a difference different people may be won. So definitely and finally is it the sole finding of the Scriptures, that the way of perfection is in tribulation, that perhaps of nothing else do we find places in the Scriptures so consistently saying the same thing, saying: "He who would serve God must prepare his soul to temptations";[1] "Through many tribulations we must enter into the kingdom of God";[2] "We are appointed" unto afflictions.[3] And so forth.

For that reason we shall not quote any particular place in the Bible, but rather rely on the strength of the impression made by the whole general doctrine of the Scriptures, that the man goes in tribulation who goes on the way of perfection; and after that we shall consider for the edification of the sufferer (for these discourses after all are on the Gospel of Our Sufferings) the joy that is in this—

[1] Ecclus. ii. 1.   [2] Acts xiv. 22.   [3] 1 Thess. iii. 3.

NOT THAT THE WAY IS NARROW, BUT THAT NARROWNESS IS THE WAY.[1]

And so by the way of perfection one goes through tribulations, and the theme of our discourse is the joy this thought holds for the sufferer. Wherefore for once our discourse does not seek to admonish anybody how he must go upon the way of tribulation, but it makes for the sufferer the joyful proclamation that tribulation is the "how", defining the way of perfection. The way in a spiritual sense is the manner of one's going. What then is the way of perfection, or, in other words, how does one go, to be on the way of perfection? One goes in tribulation. This is the first "how"? and the second is: On this way of tribulation how must one go? That this second part must never be forgotten, from start to finish, is true enough, but neither do we forget, rather we keep in mind, and the sufferer will without doubt be fortified just by this, when he has in fact discovered the joy that is in it for him, namely, that the way of perfection is through tribulations—he who being a sufferer is himself in tribulation.

Since tribulation is the way, this is the joy that is in it: THAT IT IS THEREBY *immediately* CLEAR TO THE SUFFERER, AND HE IMMEDIATELY KNOWS AS A FACT, WHAT IS REQUIRED OF HIM; SO THAT HE NEED NOT SPEND TIME, NOR USE UP ANY ENERGY, IN WONDERING WHETHER HIS TASK MIGHT NOT BE SOMETHING ELSE.

What is it enables a child, even as compared with a full-grown man, what is the reason why he is able to do what the full-grown man can scarcely do, what is it helps him and gives him an advantage? Plainly this, that the child has not the least difficulty in discovering what his task is, what he has to do—for the child has but to obey! It is the business of the parents or those who are in charge to think of the task and to consider it: as soon as the child has been told what he has to do, then

[1] Danish, *trang,* narrow or strait; *trängsel,* narrowness, tribulation.

this becomes his task. How far it may be right or wrong does not concern the child at all; not only does he not have to consider it, but he does not dare spend even a moment on that kind of consideration; on the contrary, he must obey immediately. No doubt the child compared with an adult is the weaker, but yet it is this weaker one who has a very great advantage, for the weaker, by reason of his very weakness, uses the whole of his strength in accomplishing his task, and so single-minded is he that not one moment is wasted in doubts about his task, not one ounce of strength wasted in hesitation about his task. The task is set with the imperiousness and infallibility of authority, this is the advantage, but further impetus is given to the child when it is added: Do it immediately—and so the child creates astonishment at what he does, indeed, a child can actually do what even a strong, older person can but seldom accomplish. Who has not often been surprised to see this wonder: what a child can do! When father or mother, or only the nurse, says, but says it with authority: Now go to sleep at once!—then the child sleeps. In the world we hear shallow talk of many astounding feats of men, and yet there is only one—he who was called the Only One[1]—of whom it is told that he was able to sleep at will. Or take an older, stronger person; he is in the same case as, in the opinion of the parents, the child is, he needs sleep; he says to himself, It were very well for thee to get some sleep; but is he, I wonder, really able to do as the child does, who sleeps immediately? Alas, when he would rest his head on the pillow, then likely the very opposite happens, and just then restless thoughts awake. And so, it may be, all things mingle in confusion, while now he doubts whether it is really right to sleep, and whether he is not neglecting his work, and what fears spring from that! And then again he wishes he might fall asleep but cannot. At last he says in his impatience: What is the good of lying here, when it is simply impossible to sleep? and he gets up again, but not to work, for now he can neither work nor

---

[1] Frederick the Great, known as Der Einzige.

sleep. If from the rest of sleep one is accustomed to rise up with new vigour, sometimes one may be inclined to stay in bed and refrain from rising. But with a different result, for from a vain attempt to sleep it is difficult indeed to rise; from a vain attempt to sleep one rises up indeed more tired than before.

The difficulty for an older person, which no doubt goes along with the advantage of his authority and maturity, is in this, that he has a twofold labour: he must labour to find the task and get it clearly defined, and then he must labour to achieve it. And that which proves more difficult is probably just this business of getting it quite clearly defined, getting clearly defined what the task is. And perhaps, after all, people are not so unwilling to take time and pains, and are not unequal to it—if only it be clear beyond question to them, what the task is. But the truth is, such knowledge cannot with any exactness be conveyed to them from without; it must come through the man himself. The older person, being full-grown, is supposed to be his own master. But it is the Lord and Master who has to set the task, as the parents, or whoever is responsible, do for the child, so that an older person is at once master and servant; he who shall order and he who shall obey are one and the same. Beyond question, the position is difficult, that the one to command and the one to obey should be one and the same; for it can so easily happen that the servant should get entangled in thinking about the task, and, conversely, that the master should pay too much attention to the complaints the servant utters about the difficulties involved in carrying it out. Then, alas, confusion enters, and then a man, instead of being his own master, has become unstable and irresolute and changeable, running from one thing to another, pulling down and building up, and going back to the beginning, tossed about by every breath of wind and yet not moving from the spot, until the position has at last become so utterly absurd that all his energy is spent devising new and ever newer variations of the task—as a plant that runs to seed, so runs he to feverish worry or to desires that bear no fruit. There is a sense in which he does employ much time, and take great pains, and expend much effort: all of which is as good as wasted, because there is no certain definition of the task, because there is no master—for should not he be his own master! When horses in a team have a great load to draw, how can the driver help them? Indeed he cannot pull it himself, and the driver who is not expert can lash at them, as any man might do, but the good driver, what can he do for them? He can help them instantaneously to make the supreme effort, and so with a single pull to find themselves in motion, drawing the wagon. But should the driver cause misunderstanding, taking the reins in such a way that the horses think they have only to gather themselves in readiness to pull when the sign is given —whereas the driver meant them to pull now; or should he tug the reins unevenly, so that the one horse thinks it has to pull, and the other that the driver strains the rein only in order that it may gather its energies, why then the wagon does not move from the place, even though the horses may have strength enough. But as such a sight must make us sorry, while we see that there is strength enough, but he who is master thwarts it, so too we cannot but be sorry to see the same sort of thing happen to a man. He lacks not strength, and indeed no man ever does, but he makes bad use of it, and as for him who should be master—that is, of course, the man himself— he nullifies it; for such a man will toil with scarcely a third of his strength in the right direction, and more than two-thirds in the wrong direction, against himself. Now he leaves off his work, to go back again to the beginning and consider it, and now instead of considering it he works; now he gives the wrong kind of pull to the reins, and wants to do both things at once—and all the time he does not move from where he is, but his whole life long continues, as it were, in a state of inertia, and cannot get the task so firmly fixed that it will stay fixed, while he can separate himself from this labour and still have all his strength available for the fulfilling of his task. It is not that the task becomes his burden, yet he is altogether occupied with what is burdensome: so to manipulate his task that if possible he will get it to stay fixed. It naturally follows that he never attains to bearing his burden, for he cannot even get it to stand; whenever he would, so to speak, stoop to lift his burden up, it is as if the burden toppled over, and once again he must set himself to piling it up. Alas, when we consider the lives of men, we must often say with sorrow: They do not themselves know the powers they possess, and more or less prevent themselves from finding out because with the greater part of their powers they are working against themselves!

Let us then think on the subject of our discourse more precisely. The sufferer is in distress: this is the crux of it. If only he can get a really firm grip of what his task is, then truly he will endure successfully; once he knows definitely what his task is, already much is gained. But Doubt would if possible prevent this; it would treacherously withdraw his powers, to be used towards a false objective, towards finding out what his task is, or towards thousands of speculations about what it might be. If this should happen, and Doubt prevail, if it should succeed in tricking him into fighting when he ought not to be fighting, then he must suffer defeat in his distress.

Is it not then a joyous thing that thus it comes about that tribulation is the way, since thus at once it is plain to him what his task is? For Doubt would cause the sufferer to wonder whether indeed it was impossible that tribulation should pass from him, and he should still continue in the way—without tribulation. But if tribulation is the way then indeed it is impossible that it should pass and the way remain the same. Doubt would make the sufferer wonder whether indeed it was impossible that he had missed the way, whether the very fact of tribulation did not denote that he was on the wrong way. But if tribulation is the way, then to meet tribulation on the way cannot denote that he has missed the way, but is on the contrary the very sign that he is on the right way. Doubt would make him wonder whether it was indeed impossible to go by some other way. But if tribulation is the way then it is quite impossible to go by any other way. And so about one thing there is no doubt, namely, what his task is, and not one moment nor an ounce of strength must be spent in further considering of the matter; the fact that tribulation is the way defines the task, makes certain what it is. And truly, however burdensome that tribulation be, no tribulation is so burdensome as the tribulation of the restlessness of thought in a doubt-racked, wavering soul.

Thus then the sufferer endures, going forward on perfection's way through tribulation—but more and more burdensome becomes the tribulation! This is the crux of it. But if only the task be firmly fixed, already much is gained; and may it be far from us to help to spread the lying tale that by little and little it will be easier on the narrow way, that only at the beginning is it narrow. Exactly the opposite is true, for it grows narrower and narrower. And this is easy to ascertain, if we will watch men and will see. It is perhaps more often than not that we meet a man who at some time or other has made a beginning towards willing the Good, but most men fall away just when it grows apparent that the way gets narrower instead of easier. When a man has reached the point where all his illusions vanish, about willing the Good in measure, or that in a certain measure the Good is rewarded here in the world, and when to will the Good is a really serious matter, then does the way first become really narrow, and from that point narrower and narrower. We can say nothing more right than this, if we are not with our tales to lead men astray, one minute luring them on, only the next minute to make them the more impatient. But what contains no deception, the everlasting truth, is this, that tribulation is the way. And so, once again, not one moment nor a single ounce of strength must be spent in further considering of the matter. The task is fixed. Tribulation is the way.

If anybody then would lead the sufferer to suppose that

others go the same way ever so lightly and so free of care, with no tribulations, while he goes in tribulations, then again the task stands fixed, and the sufferer has no other answer but, Tribulation is the way! May the hypocritical kind of talk be far from us that says there is so much diversity in life that by the same way some go without tribulations and through tribulations some. It can quite well happen that some should go with no tribulations, but verily he who goes with no tribulations goes not by the same way as he who goes in tribulation, for tribulation is the way. There is a prudence which, being somewhat reluctant utterly to break with the Good, is also most reluctant to give up pleasant times of dalliance and worldly gain—this prudence shows a great resourcefulness in such fictions as that there is so much diversity—not, in life, for there is no untruth in that—but that there is so much diversity on perfection's way. Let us recall the theme that was developed at the outset of our discourse, that in a spiritual sense the way consists in how one goes. See the poor wayfarer who, with feet excoriated, and wincing with pain at every step, is dragging himself along the way. Though for him there is no justification in envy, yet there is great good sense in the thought that would prompt envy, of the rich man driving past him in his luxurious carriage. For the highway is quite indifferent about the diverse ways there are of travelling on it, and it is certainly more pleasant to drive in a luxurious carriage than to travel so laboriously. But in a spiritual sense the way consists in how one goes, and surely it would be a somewhat curious thing if on the way of tribulation such a difference were found, that some might go on tribulation's way without any tribulations! And so once more the task stands firm, and the sufferer sees his task defined, for tribulation is the way. If anyone would without tribulation go, let him do so. Then he too is a traveller, but by another way, and that is his affair. But Doubt cannot take hold upon the sufferer, to make him doubtful, with the thought that others with no tribulations are going *by the same way.*

If it be true, what the proverb says, that well begun is half done, then it is also true that the fact of the task being fixed for anyone is half the doing of it, as indeed it is more than half. But since tribulation is the way, the task is fixed, and not Satan himself can succeed in insinuating a doubt about what the task is. In order to give free scope to Doubt, it would be necessary to make of the relation between tribulation and the way an accidental relation. So when a wayfarer, speaking of his way says: This way is narrow—by that he may mean there is something of chance in it, there may be another way that is not straitened, that yet leads to the same end; or else at other times the way may be easy, but just at the moment, and in these days it happens to be narrow. But if tribulation is the way, then every doubt that tribulation is his task is an attempt to find some bypath by which to go, since there is only one single way, the way of tribulation, and on that way the sufferer is. This doubt about the task resorts always to representing that there might be other ways, or that the way might be so altered that tribulation should be removed. But since tribulation is the way, then tribulation cannot be removed without the removing of the way, and there cannot be *other ways*, but only *byways*.

Is not this then a joyous thing, joyous for the sufferer, for him who finds himself on the way of tribulation, joyous, in that the least consideration is not required whether the way be the right one or no, joyous, in that he can at once begin on his task, and begin with that resolution which has the whole of its powers at command and in readiness—to endure the tribulation! For since tribulation is the way, it is no dreary cold Inevitable, nay, for he could not even wish to avoid it, since it is the way. With this in his mind the sufferer hastes to endure, nor loses a moment, nor wastes a glance in looking about him, nay, but with all his strength, full and complete, he is in the tribulation, rejoicing in tribulation, rejoicing in the thought that tribulation is the way. Granted it is not the task by itself that gives the strength, for the task is what is appointed, to the achieving of which he for whom it is appointed shall employ his strength; yet we can say too that the task gives strength. When parents understand how with their authority they should prescribe the task, when the driver knows how with his experience he should prescribe the task, it is an unspeakable help. And so too with the full-grown man; for when the task is, by the authority of the Eternal, surely established, then is it an unspeakable help towards its fulfilment. When a child is unfortunate enough to have a father who cannot command, or horses have but a poor driver, then it seems as if the child and as if the horses did not possess the half of the strength they truly have. And when a full-grown man, alas, in his suffering yields up his soul to be the sport of wavering moods, then he, in truth, is weaker than a child. But thus it is a joyous thing indeed that tribulation is the way, for it at once establishes and establishes with a certainty that cannot be shaken, what task is given a man to do.

Tribulation is the way. This then is what is joyous: THAT IT IS NOT A PECULIAR PROPERTY OF THE WAY TO BE STRAIT AND NARROW, BUT THAT IT IS A PECULIAR PROPERTY OF TRIBULATION TO BE THE WAY. AND SO IT FOLLOWS, THAT TRIBULATION MUST LEAD SOMEWHERE, THAT IT MUST BE A PRACTICABLE ROAD TO A DESTINATION, NOT BEYOND HUMAN POWER. Each of these thoughts has its own edification in defining that which is joyous, and therefore we shall dwell on each of them in turn.

IT IS NOT A PECULIAR PROPERTY OF THE WAY TO BE STRAIT AND NARROW, BUT IT IS A PECULIAR PROPERTY OF TRIBULATION TO BE THE WAY.

The closer the relation in which we set tribulation and the way, the more securely do we establish the task that is to be performed. When it is said that the way is strait and narrow, this proposition defines the way more closely; there are two concepts, to wit, the way, and that it is strait and narrow. But inasmuch as there are two concepts, it is as if a slight concession were being made to doubt, as if it might insinuate itself here between the way and the fact that it is narrow, as if doubt might stake a claim for itself, and set the sufferer wondering whether it should really be impossible for the way to exist without being narrow, or without being as narrow as it is said to be. For, whispers Doubt, the proposition must be broken up thus: the way, and then, that it is narrow.

But inasmuch as tribulation is the way, doubt perishes, and it is impossible to find any room for it. The one definition is not superior to the other; the proposition as a whole does not allow itself to be split into subject and predicate, nay, these are one and the same, that tribulation is the way, and that the way is tribulation; so closely do they belong together that doubt cannot even contrive to draw breath between them, for they are one concept; so closely do they belong together that the relation between tribulation and the way is that of things that cannot be separated. There can be no closer relation. Remove tribulation—thou removest the way; remove the way —thou removest tribulation. So closely do they belong together; so securely is the task established.

TRIBULATION MUST LEAD SOMEWHERE. For one cannot reach such a conclusion as: Because a way is narrow, therefore it must lead to something. Inasmuch as a way is a way, the just conclusion is that it must lead to something, for as soon as it ceases to lead to anything, it ceases also to be a way. The conclusion is just, inasmuch as the way is a way, but not inasmuch as it is narrow; such as addition for one who is not yet strong in faith, almost makes the proposition appear more doubtful, that that way can indeed lead to anything. But when tribulation is itself the way, then the conclusion follows: Therefore must it lead to something. For now we do not draw our conclusion from the fact of narrowness, but from the fact that it is a way.

It is our Lord's own word: Strait is the way that leads to bliss. And since he has said it, it is truly established for ever. Nor can we praise any who, wildly speculating, is bewildered. Yet if such be his case, we would—ah, how we would wish to help him, with our less perfect way of expressing the same truth—less perfect, because it is all that can be understood by anyone who has known doubt, and so can be of use to him only in the meantime, until he learn again the more perfect rule: to hold to the word of the Lord alone. That the Lord has spoken the word is truly the very surest defence against doubt, for faith, in the sense of obedience, is surer by far than even the sureness of what, in the sphere of reason, reason finds cannot be doubted. Ah, but because reason cannot doubt it, it does not follow that it is impossible for him who reasons; whether with misgiving or with defiance, for he can will to doubt. Yet, were it not our Lord's own word, that tribulation is the way, it is none the less his teaching, for does he not teach that tribulation is for our good? And so the same Lord is our warrant for that word. For a man can compass so much—clearly and with clear reasoning to develop what lies in a thought, but to give sanction to the thought is more than he can do. One with authority alone can do so, and to lend sanction to all authorities is possible only to him who is the unique authority.

So when it is said: Strait is the way that leads to bliss, this is the thought. That we find the way narrow, that tribulation is an encountering of opposition, it is an obstacle on the way; there is something to win through, but then the way does lead to bliss. Tribulation then is an *encountering of opposition, an obstacle on the way*, yet one has to win through. But since tribulation itself is the way, what wonder that one is bound to win through, what wonder that tribulation leads us somewhere! Doubt would fain deprive the sufferer of his courage, would leave him to himself in tribulation, leave him to perish in the thought, not only despondent but presumptuous, that he is forsaken of God, as though he had chanced upon a way that led only to some dead end, as though it was in a sense void of comfort that the Apostle used the words, "We are appointed to tribulations",[1] as though there were no destined purpose in tribulation, only that to tribulation were we destined.

[1] 1 Thess. iii. 3.

But when tribulation has the destined purpose of being the way, all at once there is a waft of air and the sufferer breathes again; then it must be leading somewhere, for tribulation is itself the power that bears him on. It is not one difficulty on the way, making necessary, so to speak, a fresh relay of horses, but the tribulation is itself the team, and the best there is; if only we allow it to have its will, then it helps us on, for tribulation is the way.

Is not this joyous? What limit to the confidence with which in this thought the sufferer can draw breath? He does not only commend himself to the mercy of God and go forward to meet tribulation, nay, but he says: Tribulation is to me a sign that I am well commended to him, tribulation is my aid—for tribulation is the way! As long as a child stands in awe of his teacher, doubtless he can learn much; but it is when trust has driven fear away and confidence has triumphed that the finest instruction begins. And so it is too, when the sufferer, in the assurance that tribulation is the way, has overcome tribulation; for what, in the highest sense, is it to overcome tribulation but really to believe that tribulation is the way and is our aid? The Apostle Paul says in one place: Faith is our victory,[1] and in another place: We are more than conquerors.[2] But can anybody be more than a conqueror? Yea, when before the fight begins a man has changed his enemy to be his friend. It is one thing to be a conqueror in tribulation, to overcome tribulation as one overcomes an enemy, maintaining the belief that tribulation is our enemy, but to be more than a conqueror is what it means to believe that tribulation is our friend, that it is not the opposition but the way, not the hindering but the forwarding, not making crouch but lifting up.

THE WAY OF TRIBULATION MUST BE A PRACTICABLE ROAD TO A DESTINATION. What is it that may hap upon a way to close it, so that it becomes impassable? It is tribulation, that is, straitness. But if tribulation is the way, then of a truth this way is absolutely passable. A sufferer may, if he will, suppose

---

[1] cf. 1 John v. 4.   [2] Rom. viii. 37.

his tribulation to be more and more terrifying; it makes no difference at all—this is forever sure, that tribulation is the way, and so no tribulation can be imagined that can close this way. And besides, from this it can be seen that tribulation must lead somewhere. For what else could prevent a way from leading somewhere, what else but tribulation, that is, straitness; but when on this way it cannot come to oppose our progress, then truly this way must ever be leading us somewhere.

How wonderful, that the way of tribulation is the only way without an obstacle; for tribulation itself it is that prepares the way and does not stop it! But is not this a joyous thing! For what can make a wayfarer more disconsolate than that he should have to say: Here no longer is there any way! And what, on the other hand, can make the wayfarer more joyful than that he should dare to say: Here there is always a way?

TRIBULATION IS NOT BEYOND THE SCOPE OF HUMAN POWER. Nay, but were tribulation beyond human power, then the way were closed, and tribulation would not be the way. The Apostle Paul says: "There hath no temptation taken you but such as man can bear, but God will with the temptation make also the way of escape that ye may be able to endure it."[1] But has not God made the temptation such as can be borne, since from everlasting he has so ordained that tribulation is the way? Thus tribulation is once and for all made such as can be borne. And how can it better be ensured that there be always a good escape from temptation than when tribulation is itself the way? For thus tribulation itself is always an escape, and a good escape, from tribulation.

A temptation beyond human strength would tower above a man; as a steep mountain, causing the wayfarer to despair, so would such temptation terrify the sufferer and change him into a crawling insect by comparison with the great size of temptation; like a force of nature mocking human effort, so would

---

[1] 1 Cor. x. 13 (R.V.).

such temptation, rearing itself in lofty scorn, be a proud mockery to the poor sufferer. But, God be praised! there exists not any temptation that is beyond human strength; it is a lying tale, invented by a timid or a cunning man who would fain repudiate the guilt, would diminish the guilt by magnifying the temptation, would justify himself by making it something beyond human strength. Scripture says just the opposite; it not only says that there exists not any temptation that is beyond human strength, but also says in another place, where it speaks of such a terror, in the expectation of which men shall be fainting, to the faithful it says: "When these things begin to come to pass, then lift up your heads."[1] Thus temptation has not a more than human magnitude; altogether to the contrary, when tribulation is most terrible, the believer is higher by a head—higher by a head? truly he is so much higher by the very head that he lifts above his tribulation! And since tribulation is the way, a believer is in fact above his tribulation, for the way on which a man is travelling does not, surely, go over his head, nay rather, when he is following it, he treads it under foot.

And so this thought holds for us pure joy, the thought that tribulation is the way. A sufferer knows definitely and at once what his task is, he can start on it at once with all his strength; no doubt can insinuate itself between the way and tribulation, because they are forever inseparable; hence it is forever certain that this way must lead him somewhere, seeing that no tribulation here can bar the way, the way being always practicable, and tribulation never beyond the scope of human power. Only it must never for a moment be forgotten, and it must be here repeated in conclusion, that the other question still remains, of how the sufferer has to walk upon the way of tribulation. Ah, but if it be true that it is small profit to a man to cling with cold heart to a dead persuasion: in very truth that persuasion which makes a man joyful and radiant in tribulation shall also make him strong for what comes

[1] Luke xxi. 26, 28.

next, namely, to go as he ought to go on tribulation's way. And thus to believe, with a confident spirit, and without any doubt, that the tribulation in which one finds oneself is the way—is not this in truth to go as one ought to go on tribulation's way?

VI

Before a man begins on anything, whether he has to act or has to suffer, first of all he makes the calculation, can he in action raise up the tower and how high; can he in suffering find strength to lay the foundations of it and how deep? That is to say, he makes a calculation of his powers and his task, and this he *weighs up* in his mind.

To weigh up is a figure of speech but a most significant one. And so we find it to be, like every figure of speech, of profit to us, when as through a secret door, suddenly, by a sort of magic, we are transported from the most commonplace situation to stand amidst the loftiest conceptions, and even while we speak of common familiar things discover all at once that we are speaking also of the ultimate sublime.

To weigh up is an image of weighing: the balance weighs, or, on the balance we weigh. But what, in fact, is weighing? It is to state an exact relation between two quantities, or to make an exact statement of that relation. So much for the balance. To the balance it is a matter of sheer exactness which of the two weighs more, it merely states the weight, and is not partial either to the one or to the other side. This is just what we value in a balance, saying when it is like this that it is a good or an accurate balance. And we could not well speak of a balance any other way, unless perhaps when we should say that for this weighing there is no need of art, that art first begins when there is partiality for the one or the other side: and so there is force—aye, let us use the vulgar but so expressive mode of speech—there is force in the saying: Keep a balanced tongue in your head.

The balance then is used for weighing, but man weighs up; that is to say, he does more than weigh in the sense of the balance, he weighs up; being above the weighing, superior to mere measuring by weight, for he chooses. Therefore we may say with truth that the figure of weighing, if only we hold on to it, will lead us at length to what is essential in human nature, to what constitutes it, and to what makes it superior. For as, in order to weigh, there must be two quantities, so also with the man who weighs up; inasmuch as, merely in order that he may be able to weigh, he must be so constituted as to possess two quantities. And so indeed it is, for man is compounded of the temporal and the eternal. Time and eternity are in a spiritual sense the quantities to be weighed. But if he is to weigh up, the man himself must also either have or be a third in relation to those two quantities. This is Choice: he weighs, he weighs-up, he chooses. Yet there is one case that can never occur, though it might possibly occur with the balance, namely that the proportion should be indicated to be equal, the two quantities weighing equally as much. Nay this, let God be praised, can never be, for the eternal, rightly understood, is already higher in the scale, and any who will not grasp this fact can never come to weighing-up.

Thus, ere he begins, thus, at the beginning of life, does a man weigh up. So far he has but little of experience, but little of an intimate knowledge of the temporal; only in imagination does he have a picture of the temporal and of the eternal, and he makes a choice between them. Ah, we may almost dare to say with confidence of every man, that thus in the beginning did it appear to him, that once upon a time it was to him so obvious, that the eternal outweighs the temporal; yea, not only was it obvious to him, but it moved him deeply, touched his inmost soul: and that perhaps is why so often the youth's first choice is made not without fervent tears.

Yet that does not by any means settle everything. For just as it is little help to a man to have an impersonal knowledge of the relation between the temporal and the eternal, so is this first choice of little avail if it be not repeated again and again —and perhaps it must be repeated under very different conditions! The youth has grown older, life weighs heavy on him, and now he is—for we would fain hasten from what is lighter

H

to be able all the longer to dwell on the theme of these discourses, the gospel of our sufferings—now he is a sufferer. Then must he, if continual weighing-up is not to be a waste of his time and a dissipating of his energies, turn back to weighing, once more seriously weigh, and so weigh-up. The weight of the temporal he knows. Does the eternal still in truth weigh heavier? So he asks himself, but also he asks others; lest he should waste his time and dissipate his energies in much talk with one and another, he makes earnest enquiry of one who is tried in counsel. And, let God be praised, such counsellors are in truth to be found, such witnesses, if not among the living then among the dead, and first and foremost in the Holy Scriptures. So perchance he reads in the Apostle Paul these words:

For our light affliction which is but for a moment, worketh for us a far more exceeding and eternal weight of glory (2 Cor. iv. 17).

These words we shall at this time take for the basis of our edification, considering the joy there is for a sufferer in this:

THAT EVEN WHEN TEMPORAL SUFFERING WEIGHS DOWN MOST HEAVILY, YET THE BLESSEDNESS OF THE ETERNAL WEIGHS UP TO MORE.

But before we go on to consider the words of the Apostle at greater length, there is one observation that must first be made, which may seem to be an obvious inference, but which, in the light of our experience of men's lives, well deserves to have attention drawn to it. For it is quite obvious that if there is to be any meaning in these words just spoken, assuring a man that even when temporal suffering weighs down most heavily, the blessedness of the eternal weighs up to more, then he himself must weigh it in the balance, must in fact see to it that this counter-weight of the eternal is given his full consideration. This is of course quite obvious, and if it were also obvious that every man did so then every man would truly have assurance of the preponderating blessedness of the eternal. For if only this thought itself is taken quite seriously, then in the balance it must prove to be the overweight. Ah, but perhaps it happens only rarely, that anybody does thus rightly weigh. Yet in the world, time and again, day in and day out, from morn till eve, there is endless talk of weighing-up and weighing-up, and still it stands that he who does not have in his mind, as the other quantity in the balance, the thought of the eternal, weighs up nothing and is not even capable of weighing-up. For the weighing-up of one thing that is temporal against another, leaving out the eternal, is not weighing-up; it is fooling oneself, it is throwing away one's time; and so, cheated by life's trivialities, one throws away the chance of everlasting bliss. Here again it appears how much is implied in the common figure of weighing-up. The fundamental significance of our human weighing-up is in balancing what is temporal against what is eternal; in every other weighing-up by men this fundamental significance must be present, else the weighing-up in spite of all our busy-ness and all our inflated self-importance, has no foundation, nor has it any meaning.

But do men, we may ask, in truth so live, as always seriously to take into consideration the thought of the eternal? There is a busy-ness, a busy effort to obtain, and busy discussion of, the necessities of life, such a busy-ness as appears to have altogether forgotten what is the one thing needful. And yet if thou dost associate with such busy ones thou wilt ever hear them talk of weighing-up and weighing-up, although they have utterly forgotten what is the fundamental significance of weighing-up. As for the more fortunate, the favourite of fortune, he is but too easily persuaded and fooled by the temporal, and it seems to him that he is so prosperous as to need nothing more; or if, in spite of all, he seems to himself to be not really prospering, he is still so fooled by the temporal that it never enters his head to seek the reason where he ought. And yet if thou dost associate with such a man, him too thou wilt ever hear talk of weighing-up and weighing-up, although it is easy for thee to discover how utterly he too has forgotten what is most profoundly significant. It may be, alas, that there are many who live like this, who even call themselves Christians, although what is distinctive of fundamental Christianity is just that fundamental significance of weighing-up. It may be there are many who live thus fooled by the temporal. Let me use a simple illustration to make their condition plain.

When on a dark but starry night the prosperous man drives comfortably in his carriage with the lamps alight—why, then he feels secure and fears no difficulty, for he carries his own light with him, and it is not dark about him. But just because he has his lamps alight, and the light is strong about him, just because of this he cannot see the stars at all. His lamps hide the stars, of which the poor peasant, driving with no lights, can have the splendid vision, in the night dark but clear with stars. And thus they live who are befooled by the temporal; either, being obsessed with the necessities of life, they are too busy to win the vision beyond, or else, in their prosperity and times of ease they have, as it were, their lamps alight, they have around them and close about them, everything so reassuring and bright and comfortable—but the vision is not there, the vision beyond, the vision of the stars!

No doubt such people cheat themselves. Yet they have no intention of cheating others, whether with blind or with blinding guidance (for the blinding light of the temporal is always just as dangerous as the blind guidance of the dark). But there are also some who, rashly deceiving themselves, would rashly teach men so. They would do away with this notion of eternity and eternal blessedness altogether, and by all sorts of cunning inventiveness in whatever is made for comfort and for ease would teach men to surround themselves with the greatest brightness possible in things temporal, till it become impossible to see eternity at all. Or if they would not altogether do away with eternity yet they would so far belittle it that it comes about at last that there is no eternal difference—can anything be more ridiculous!—between time and eternity. What then can the difference be? Surely it must be plain beyond all contradiction that as there is between the human and the animal the difference of humanity, so between the temporal and the eternal there is the difference of eternity; or could the difference amount to this, that there is not any difference, or can the eternal to all eternity know any difference save that it is eternal? Such false teachers cannot simply be called Pharisees, but, what is worse, *either* on the one hand the Pharisee who points out the right way accurately but in fact does not tread it himself, the Pharisee whose words, that is to say, I can take seriously and act upon, leaving to God, what never can be my concern, to judge the hypocrite; *or*, on the other hand, the so-called genuine guide who genuinely treads himself the way he recommends to others, but, note well, perverts the way, and, counselling others, goes in company with them on a wild wandering way.

Now take the sufferer: when he neglects to give serious consideration to the notion of eternity and eternal blessedness, when feeling the weight of his suffering, he does not weigh the blessedness at all, what wonder is it that his temporal suffering tips the scales, what wonder is it that he finds it heavy, so heavy! Ah, when eternity at length shall weigh the man, doubtless it will find him under weight, for in thus becoming heavier he comes the nearer to being found by eternity too light. Or if, for once, the sufferer does take the thought of eternity, as it were, in his hand, to feel its weight, but finds its weight is small, what wonder if his temporal suffering outweighs it quite! Then when the very next moment the sufferer careless throws that thought of eternity away, what wonder that he finds his suffering then still heavier, heavy to the point of despair, since not only does his suffering weigh him down, but he adds his own heaviness to his suffering with the rash thought that God has abandoned him—having himself abandoned the eternal! What wonder if such a sufferer, alas, should in the end seek the last desperate way of escape, and want to make an end of his agony—make a beginning of that which in eternity is waiting for him?

From which mournful contemplation let us now pass on to consider the words we have read of the Apostle: for Paul was truly the man who knew how to weigh and to weigh-up; of a truth, if in the mouth of Christ was found no guile, then neither was there any false weight with his Apostle.

"Our distress, which is brief and light, gains us a surpassingly great, an eternal weight of glory."[1] Distress, that is, *gains* a surpassingly great, an eternal weight of glory. But if distress at every moment—and also, that is to say, if all temporal suffering—most heavily weighing us down *gains us such a weight of glory; then blessedness preponderates indeed.* For that by which something is gained, the means of acquiring something, is, as it stands to reason, the thing of lesser worth, and what is gained the higher. It is so easy to understand this, and it is a conception so generally accepted, and yet so deeply grounded, that we regard it as a most deplorable, a most detestable confusion, when any would reverse the case and cause the object to be sought, what is itself the aim, to be the means, would make of truth, for example, a means, in the service of greed for money, the yearning of ambition, or other evil passions. The moral order, which is concerned with the question what by itself and in itself is the aim, shows us the means to be inferior to the aim. Yea, even if something worldly be the aim, and some other worldly thing the means, the means in relation to the aim is still inferior (although there is a sense in which both aim and means may be of equally little value, being both worldly). Thus when anybody with his money gains some worldly good, he esteems his money as of less account than the good he gains with it for himself; while again perhaps he esteems his money as the aim, and something else of a worldly nature as the means and so of less account, by which he is able to gain money.

But a surpassingly great, an *eternal* weight of glory, is no

---

[1] 2 Cor. iv. 17. We give here the Danish version of the text, in order that the allusions that follow may be more evident (trans.).

worldly good; this aim cannot just chance to be the higher and the means the lower value; nor can the case so vary that at one time this good is the aim and then again the means by which another good is to be won. So if suffering *gains* the good, then quite simply and literally it is outweighed by blessedness, even when suffering presses down most heavily. The other good is so infinitely higher than the means, that even in suffering's heaviest hour the sense that it is gaining a surpassingly great, an eternal weight of glory, makes blessedness outweigh it. He who will not understand and will not believe this has himself to blame, for in suffering's heaviest hour he lets this sense be extinguished, the sense of that which suffering gains.

For when is the weight of temporal suffering most terrible upon a man? Is it not when it seems to him to have no meaning, to win nothing, to gain nothing? Is it not when suffering, as he in his impatience might express it, is without sense or reason? Take one who resolves to struggle in a competition; does he complain though to prepare for it may mean great effort, does he complain even though it may mean much pain and hardship? And wherefore does he not complain? Because one who even while making an uncertain venture yet knows or thinks he knows, that his suffering will bring him the award of victory, just when the effort is greatest and most painful rallies the manhood in him with the thought of the award, the thought that it is his suffering that will serve to win it for him. How much of suffering will not man endure when he knows that by it he will gain a livelihood, or gain the honour or the wealth, the prize of love or whatever it might be! But the truth is that a man's mind can still grasp just so much, or the man thinks that he can grasp it; a man knows or at least he thinks he knows that his suffering gains him that which he desires—which he desires, alas, though it be so infinitely less in worth than a weight of glory surpassingly great. When on the other hand, suffering so overwhelms a man that his reason will no longer cope with all his suffering because reason cannot comprehend what can be gained by suffering; when the sufferer cannot comprehend anything of this dark reckoning, neither the cause of his suffering, nor the intention in it, neither why he of all others should be thus oppressed, nor what purpose it holds of benefit to himself —and then, in his weakness feeling that he cannot throw off his suffering, rebels and throws off his faith, and will not believe that suffering gains him anything: why then it is certain that blessedness will not outweigh it, then it is quite left out of the man's account.

But if the sufferer holds fast to what no doubt the mind cannot comprehend but to which faith clings—that suffering gains a surpassingly great, an eternal weight of glory; then blessedness outweighs it, and then the sufferer not only bears his suffering but knows that blessedness outweighs it. The insight that can recognise that suffering gains something confers a temporal endurance: but a faith, in despite of understanding, that suffering, apparently nothing else but pain and useless trouble, is gaining him a surpassing and eternal weight of glory, confers the endurance that endures for ever. Whereas sometimes a sufferer finds the distress in which he is can be endured, and yet has his misgivings and fears lest the next moment it should become beyond endurance: on the other hand this is true, that there is available to everyone who suffers another kind of reassurance than the treacherous one that treacherously hangs its argument upon any human assumption, this, namely, the will to believe that the heaviest suffering is winning an immeasurably great, an eternal weight of glory.

And so, even when temporal suffering weighs most heavily, blessedness still weighs more. In what sense the Apostle says suffering *gains* that glory we shall not now further develop, for it has no bearing on the theme of our discourse. Only let this be remembered, that it cannot be in any sense of deserving. For in that case it would have to be within the capacity of the understanding that suffering gains blessedness, and then again blessedness would have to be within the capacity of the understanding, since one could understand it as something deserved. But just so our discourse would not be of an eternal blessedness, since eternal blessedness can only be believed in, and just for that reason cannot be earned. We shall not, however, pursue any further such an unfolding. But this still stands fast: that suffering gains a surpassingly great, an eternal weight of glory—thus blessedness, turns the balance.

"Our distress, *which is brief and light*, gains us . . ." But if the distress is light and brief, then it is quite evident that the blessedness outweighs it, and so there is no need to say a single word more, for a distress which is brief and light, and which, moreover, gains a great eternal weight of glory, can never be weighty in the balance, we may rather say indeed that it has no weight at all, compared with this great weight of glory. However impatient the sufferer, he would admit this, but at the same time hold the opinion that nothing was proved by it, especially about his own suffering, for his own suffering is so far from being brief and light that it is quite unspeakably heavy and prolonged. This being so, our discourse has got itself into a quandary. And yet not so; it has a special affection for these apostolic words, our distress, which is brief and light. Elsewhere I have tried to develop what is no doubt familiar to all, how truly and how emphatically the Apostle Paul may be described as one tried in almost all human suffering, one tried to the uttermost. Here I must put it more shortly, and I know nothing more significant to say on the subject than this: that Paul was no sheltered and pampered individual. The impatient man must not allow himself to be deceived by appearances and think that it is a spoiled child of fortune who is speaking of a mere half-hour's distress. The meaning in the apostolic words is not put quite directly, but somewhat like this it is: In faith I wait for such surpassingly great, such an eternal weight of glory, the blessedness of eternity for me is such a good, that in comparison I call thirty years of every kind of suffering a distress that is brief and light. Consider! this is apostolic language; for many a fatuous eulogy is heard, of the blessedness of eternity, that with flowery words and ravishing description would play tricks with the senses—the kind of thing an apostle does not understand, but what he understands to be the best eulogy of eternal bliss is that it is such a good that when he speaks of it his contemplation of it makes him call his sufferings a distress both brief and light.

So, it is by comparison that thirty years' suffering is made a distress that is brief and light. But to compare is also to weigh. Only, comparing does not so weigh as to keep the two quantities at a distance and apart from one another, but on the contrary brings them so close together that the presence of blessedness changes the way we speak of distress. It is because the thought of blessedness is there, because blessedness is there, that the Apostle speaks as he does of distress. Which is quite as it ought to be. Does not the presence of the King make us speak of the same matters in quite a different way from the way we should speak at other times? Of such a misfortune as at other times would vex us and make us grumble in our own room, we say in the presence of the King: Your Majesty, it is a thing of no consequence. The presence of our beloved makes us speak in a different way about the same matters from the way we should speak at other times. Of what would usually upset and disturb us we say in the presence of our beloved: My dear, it is a trifle. And this changing of one's way of speaking, and especially one's way of behaving, we call the respect of the subject for the majesty of the King, we call it the joyful state of being in love, we call it reverence with reference to what is most to be revered, and in the more ordinary case, politeness. From first to last of it, politeness consists in taking note that somebody is present, and who it is who is present. As for the blessedness of eternity and its presence in our thought of it: alas, how often in regard to it a sufferer is, not to put it more harshly, so impolite as not to heed it, to behave as if it were not there—for in thought it can be always there.

But yet the blessedness weighs most. The sufferer who

attends to speaking the court-language of heaven recognises that it weighs the most. Luther has somewhere said that a Christian must wear the court-dress of the cross; but should he not also, I ask, be proficient in using, and use, the court-language of heaven, and speak it out of the depths of his heart? For, as we have said, pouring forth facile words on the glory of bliss is but empty and worthless speech; but with lips tight-pressed as it were, not talking freely of bliss, yet speaking of life's distresses in quite an altered way, so as to show that one is speaking of bliss: that is the language of the court.

But only from the depths of the heart is it spoken, for this language of the heavenly court contains no falsehood, as sometimes we rightly imply-court-language to be but flattering falsehood; it is no such manner of speech as court-language commonly is; nay, but it is nothing more or less than a way of thinking. And so it is quite literally true, as the Apostle says, that this distress of ours is brief and light. Or is seventy years really an eternity; or is not a mere seventy years but a brief space over against eternity? And must it not be light when with it there is borne to us an expectation of the surpassing weight of glory, should it not be light just in the measure that the great weight makes it light? If distress is not light, yet what does even the heaviest suffering weigh against an eternal weight of glory? For the question is not what the heaviest suffering weighs, but what it weighs against an eternal weight of glory.

So blessedness turns the scales; and all that is required of us is that we should be faithful to such a conception of the blessedness of eternity, recognising that it turns the scales, in order that always, whatever our suffering, we may be unchanging in speaking of unchanging eternity. As soon as anyone changes his mind then it is not blessedness but the sufferer who has changed. Consider! One who would serve a cause just so far as it serves him changes his mind a great deal; and one who would love a maid just so far as his purpose is served changes his mind with changing fortune. Such a double-minded man speaks now, falsely, of having the honour to serve the cause, and again, as a traitor, he will not accept the shame of serving it; now he speaks as a flatterer about the honour of being loved, and again with a face of brass repudiates—this shame! But a humble man, inspired to espouse a cause that he loves, knows that the cause stays still the same, that it stays the unchanged cause that he has the honour to serve; and not only does not abandon it, not only suffers all for it, nay, but is ever aware of the honour it is to suffer, to suffer for this same cause. He never forgets, what is known to enthusiasm, that he holds a relation of honour to the cause for which he stands; whether he conquers or suffers has nothing whatever to do with it; the relation remains unchanged, and he has the honour to conquer in service of the cause, or he has the honour to suffer in service of the cause. Or is not he the true magnanimous faithful courtier who goes with a fallen emperor into exile, and, when the imperial majesty is clad in poverty, still with the same deference and homage says, as once in the palace halls: Your Majesty!—because it was not by the purple that he knew the emperor, to cringe before him, and therefore in his magnanimity can recognise him in his rags.

And so also with the good that is the blessedness of eternity. Faithfulness is, while all things change, to think and speak of it the same, not in time's pleasant easy days to flatter and be loud in praise of this good thing, and then in the day of suffering, faithless to the eternal and self-deceiving, to change one's tune. Alas! for the difference lies in this, that it would grieve the emperor, were the courtier to change, but let none suppose the blessedness of eternity to suffer, through any in his faithlessness being traitor to himself. Therefore, if a man has known but little of distress in life, there is only one thing to say about the blessedness of heaven; but if he be tried in all manner of sufferings, again there is only one thing to say, for this good abides, it is not changed by suffering, but changes on the contrary the heaviest suffering to a distress which is brief and light.

Is not this an outweighing? *Is it not even such an outweighing that suffering cannot in fact be weighed in the balance along with the eternal weight of glory,* since there is needed no great weight of the blessedness of eternity, but the least part of it is a great and eternal weight! And this also is implied in the words of the Apostle. Our distress, that is, this temporal distress, which is brief and light, gains an eternal weight: but then not only does this give to blessedness an overweight, but such is the relation that the two quantities cannot be weighed against each other. Let us understand one another. It is proverbial that a pound of gold and a pound of feathers weigh the same, and this of course is true; but no doubt we should add that in another, more important, sense the two quantities cannot be weighed against each other, and why not?—because the balance cannot show the one pound to be gold, the other feathers, and because gold has a special value which plainly makes the weighing of gold and feathers against each other meaningless. And that is how it is also with the two quantities we have in mind. The difference is not the difference between blessedness and suffering, but the difference between *eternal* blessedness and *temporal* suffering. The relation between them is one of disparity, and that there is a disparity is most distinctly shown by this, that the relation between temporal happiness and eternal blessedness is the same disparity, and that temporal happiness can be reckoned as nothing in comparison with eternal blessedness. So also and in the very same way can temporal suffering be reckoned. Not only are temporal suffering and eternal blessedness different in quality, as gold and feathers are essentially different in quality, but they are different with the essential difference of the infinite; the least part of the blessedness of eternity weighs infinitely more than the most prolonged earthly suffering.

Oh, how unspeakable, how surpassingly great this joy! Oh, that the sufferer would indeed realise it, would believe it, and would know that even when suffering weighs most heavily blessedness still outweighs it; that the sufferer would strike a true balance; yea, more than that, so that not only he sinks not under the weight of his suffering, but rather is faint from the weight of his bliss, and so that with foretaste of bliss he breaks, so to speak, the balance in pieces and says: Here is no question of weighing at all! But how seldom a man is found in the world like this, how utterly different it is in the world! This is not said to challenge joyousness, which is the theme of our discourse, but it is said that we may if we can challenge the sadness which is the state of but too many. How many are there not, who live in such a way that without thinking they agree that blessedness turns the scales, and without thinking they agree that eternal blessedness is something disparate with our temporal being; in other words, they let the thought be put aside, and let it stand for what it is worth, but do not occupy themselves with it at all—so disparate for them has eternity's blessedness become from their lives' temporal aims; they live in the lazy notion that we shall all be surely saved, so great for them has the disparity of blessedness become. What a change were there, if it should be that the heaviest suffering of a long life for once appeared to reckon as nothing compared with the blessedness of eternity; if for once it should be that he who not only walked bravely amid all temporal dangers but was so brave as almost to refuse to acknowledge them as danger, that such a man in fear and trembling should work out his salvation! And what were lost by such a change? For what gave the Romans so much courage in battle, but that they had learned to fear worse things than death! But what gave the believer amid the dangers of life on earth, a quite different kind of courage from that of any Roman, what but that he knew not only a greater danger but also an eternal blessedness! And what makes our generation so fearful, even in the dangers of earthly life, what, but that it does not know the supreme danger! And what is our generation's greatest guilt, what, but that it does not heed eternity's blessedness! Shall men escape the punishment? Does not Scripture say: "How then shall those escape [the punishment] those who neglect so great salvation?"[1]

But it is far from being the purpose of our discourse to pass judgment, it would only have men judge differently; our discourse seeks but to proclaim the gospel of our sufferings, which neither has the speaker himself invented nor does he consider he deserves credit for proclaiming—for this it is too joyous! Possibly one might get credit for proclaiming this or that temporal truth; but the truth of eternity and the joy of its blessedness are too joyous to allow room for the poor reckoning of merit. If a man in pure sacrifice, in the heaviest suffering, went on incessantly proclaiming this joy, he would still earn no merit thereby, because what is joyous is this, that even when temporal suffering weighs most heavily the blessedness outweighs it. A temporal truth must consent to keep an account with those who proclaim it; but the blessedness of eternity holds a receipt in full, which makes a reckoning unthinkable, for even when suffering weighs most heavily blessedness still of a truth outweighs it.

[1] Heb. ii. 3.

VII

From fear of men, from considerations of worldly gain, to be so cowardly and base as not to dare acknowledge the object of his love before the world, is surely about the most hateful and despicable charge that can be laid against a man; and this charge, that from fear of men, from considerations of worldly gain, a man should be so cowardly and base as not to dare acknowledge his faith and the object of his faith in the world —this is the most despicable charge that can be laid against him.

Even, therefore, if it were not, as it is, the case, that the Holy Scriptures most solemnly teach, as required of such as make a Christian confession (and what is required is already said in calling them confessors), that they should acknowledge their faith before the world; and even if it were not true that Christ has said: Whosoever shall deny me before men, him will I also deny before my Father which is in heaven—even were it not so, yet would it follow as a mere matter of course, follow from the intense inward urge in the Christian, that so he ought to do.

And again. Although it is commanded, and is stressed with all the emphasis of eternity, yet if the confession is not a consequence of that inmost urge, then such a confession is not what is required. So that if any were so bold as deliberately to deceive himself and think it most expedient, seeing that it was required of him, think it most expedient, with a view to the judgment of eternity, that he should confess Christ, then such a man not only does not confess Christ, but misrepresents him in a sacrilegious manner, as if Christ were a vain imperious being who aspired to a great name in the world. Nay, not for this has Christ required the confession, and not thus has he required it. On the contrary, he has in fact required that in his followers there shall be that depth of inwardness that will make confession issue as a matter of course—if it should be required; for that inwardness can be silent too, and equally well-pleasing to God, but the same inwardness can never be silent—when the confession is required! Yea, how indeed should faith become so strong in any man as that he should have faith unto salvation, so strong and so disinterested in this sense (for this is probably the most difficult form of disinterestedness, to have no regard to one's own ideas of gain and to the fertile excuses of one's passions, nor yet to the fearful bodings of a terror-struck imagination, in the consciousness of sin—yet without such disinterestedness one cannot believe unto salvation!)—were faith itself not strong enough, disinterested enough, to dare to make confession—if confession be required.

Hence every true Christian has always been willing, when required, to confess his faith; he has not—and it is just this that is to be praised—he has not vaingloriously asserted himself to seek the opportunity, but rather with a burning eagerness of spirit has sought to assure himself that honestly and before God he was willing to do it when required. Thus was it once upon a time when Christianity was in a world of paganism, and the Christian in everything was challenged to confess his faith before the world, for *to confess one's faith was the same thing as to preach Christianity*. Then truly men were eager and prepared to make confession, and Christians of that day held it in high esteem, so that although the same faith was acknowledged by them all, yet some especially they called confessors, who had not, to be sure, as martyrs sacrificed their lives, but yet were tried in the many dangers that went with their confession. In those days it was required of all without exception to confess. For what did the world want, and what would it force those Christians to confess, but that they were not Christians! The pagan world would treat those Christians as evildoers, yet what was wanted of them (as several of the fathers of the Church have so clearly and so penetratingly propounded) was not what was wanted of a criminal, to acknowledge and confess his guilt; nay, quite the reverse, for what was required of the Christian was to confess that he was not a Christian.

But have not circumstances altered now—now, when Christianity has prevailed and is victorious, now, when all men are Christians, now, when the last demand to be made is to confess that one is not a Christian (which would unquestionably be the best of claims to be one)? Let us calmly and soberly consider the matter. For if it be God that giveth the spirit of power and might, then it is the same God that giveth "the spirit of a sound mind"; and though base cowardice and the fear of men are at all times equally to be detested, yet the exaggerations of enthusiasm and "a zeal without knowledge" are no less pernicious, and in their motive may even be at times just as detestable and as great a sacrilege. When among pagans a Christian confesses Christ, his act of confession is the same thing as the proclaiming of Christianity before those who do not know it. Such a confession holds no judgment on the pagans for not being Christians, for pagans do not give themselves out to be Christians. But when, on the other hand, the Christian lives among Christians, or among people all of whom call themselves Christians, then to confess Christ is not the same thing as to proclaim Christianity (since those to whom the confession is addressed have been taught Christianity and call themselves Christians); but it is a judgment of others, a judgment of those who *say* they are Christians, that they are only *giving themselves out* to be Christians, therefore a judgment that they are not Christians, and therefore a judgment, at its mildest, for levity and thoughtlessness, at its severest, for hypocrisy.

These two situations are no doubt very different and easy to distinguish, since in the one case the Christian is surrounded by pagans and so to be a Christian is just the same as confessing Christ, whereas in the other case the Christian who makes a Christian confession is surrounded by Christians who also make a Christian confession, and so if he would go further in confessing Christ he is refusing to acknowledge the Christianity of the others.

And now let me use a simple concrete example, for clarity's

sake, to illustrate the theme. If there were some foodstuff, some article of diet, which one way or another had so great significance for a man that it moved his deepest feelings (we might suppose some national food, or a food with religious significance), and if in consequence he could not ever tolerate that it should be laughed at or so much as referred to with contempt, then it would naturally follow that if this occurred where he was present he would assert himself and make known his feelings. But let us suppose the situation somewhat altered. The man now is in company with some others and this food is brought in. As it is being served, each of the guests says, "This is the finest and choicest of foods". But the man in question discovers to his amazement, or thinks he discovers, that the guests are not partaking of this dish, they let it go past them untouched, and keep to other dishes, while yet they say that this dish is the finest and the choicest. In such a case is the man called on to assert his own conviction? Indeed there is none to contradict him, none who says anything but what he says. So if he hereupon does solemnly protest his feelings, then *either*: there is no sense in his behaviour—inasmuch as it is senseless when all the rest are saying the same thing to affirm his conviction along with their unanimous conviction, for this is not to confess but to join in agreement; *or else*: he will be passing the judgment on the others that they do not mean what they say.

And so it is also with the confessing of Christ among people who say of themselves that they are Christians—if we keep in mind the defect in our illustration, for on the material level you can make sure whether a man eats or does not eat of the dish he praises so highly, whereas in things spiritual it is in truth only the Searcher of hearts who can know how far a man does not mean what he says. It is quite possible a Christian should discover to his amazement, or think he discovers, that many people who all say to be a Christian is the highest good, and they themselves are Christians, do yet appear to care extremely little for this highest good. But if he uses this as an opportunity to confess Christ, then his confession is not a proclamation of Christianity, but it is—a judgment on others! Confession, in the sense in which the Bible and the Church use the word, suggests opposition, suggests that there is one who contradicts. But here it was not so; he thought, on the contrary, he had discovered there were many contradicting themselves, or not meaning what they said. And so he confesses Christ not as against those who deny Christ, but as against those who also confess Christ; and that is to say, he passes judgment on the others that their confession is an untruth; it implies, not that their words are untrue, for indeed they speak truth, but that the true words lack truth *in them*. Whether any be called upon so to confess Christ as to refuse him to others who yet affirm the same as he does, is quite another question, and for the answer to it one may not directly appeal to primitive Christianity; it is quite another question, which no doubt it were well that everyone should consider seriously. For no matter what the answer may be, it can never be such that from it might follow an exemption from doing all that he can to help other men in their Christian faith. But this is not confessing Christ, this teaching, guidance, exhortation of others with whom he has that one thing in common, joining with them in a general confession of Christianity. In the days when Christianity was at war with a paganism denying Christ, and when every Christian was called to confess Christ before the world, no doubt it would never occur to the Christians as a community to confess Christ among themselves, because the individual Christian who in that fellowship would take upon himself to confess Christ, would be presuming to deny that the others were Christian. Therefore this must always be borne in mind, that what, while Christianity is surrounded by paganism, amounts to a proclamation of Christ, within the Christian community so easily becomes sectarian self-sufficiency and arrogance.

And yet it by no means follows from what has just been propounded, which amounts but to a recognition of the care that is needed, that the occasion can never arise in the midst of a nominal Christianity when a man may be put to the necessity of confessing Christ. But on this we shall reach no decision, only leaving it to the serious self-examination of each individual; nor do we bring it forward for consideration as if the theme of our discourse were the confessing of Christ. Nay, we bring now to mind the supreme example of conflict for the sake of a conviction, in order that from the greatest we may learn for the lesser conflict, in order that we may in whatever fight for a conviction is allotted to us learn how to fight aright. For even if this does not happen, and a man's life does not lead him into the difficulty of the conflict in which he must confess Christ, yet there are other ways as well in which he may be brought to the point of decision, when he must assert, and knows he is bound to assert, a standpoint involving, and integral with, his deepest conviction. And of this too it is true to say that from fear of other men, from considerations of worldly gain, to be so cowardly and base as not to dare acknowledge his conviction is the most hateful and despicable thing that can be said of a man. Hence it is good to be well prepared, and well aware beforehand of the difficulties, so that one may be resolute in danger, and yet familiar too with the joyous thought of the courage that is our guide.

More and more, alas, as a certain superficial culture spreads, and the variety of interests linking one man with another increase in number, more and more as envy and fear, engendered by the pettiness of incessant comparison, gain ground like a plague, it is unhappily as if all things were directed towards the suffocating of the courage of mankind. At the same time as there is a struggle to overthrow dictatorships and oppressions, it seems as if there were an all-out labouring to develop the most dangerous servitude: a man in his petty outlook fearing his fellow-men. Ah, but a tyrant (if indeed there be any such, and it be not but an ancient fable revived for the sake of the heroic achievement of overthrowing him), a tyrant can in truth be overthrown, for at him it is at least possible and even easy to take aim. And the fear of man when that means rulers and the powerful is indeed an ancient story: at least they are many who in this sense fight against danger—and the danger is probably of little account! For one with no experience might in his innocence arrive at the conclusion that the danger against which many fight must surely be a great danger, since there are so many who fight; whereas those somewhat more experienced reach what may be a truer conclusion thus: the danger against which many fight is hardly a great danger—because there are many, and a multitude is what one looks for last of all where a great danger is to be fought! But that evil spirit, the fear of man which springs from pettiness in the relation of a man to his fellow-men, and the tyranny of man over his fellows, that evil spirit which one conjures up for oneself, nor does it dwell in any single individual, nor is it any single individual, but it hides and prowls around to seek its prey, insinuating itself into the relations between man and man: that evil spirit that would do away indeed with every man's relation to his God, is very difficult to exterminate.

We are scarcely aware of the fact that it is servitude we are cultivating: we forget it in our zeal to liberate mankind by overthrowing the dictatorships. We are scarcely aware that it is servitude: how could it be that we are slaves in relation to our fellow-men? Yet we are taught, quite rightly, that if a man unfree is dependent on anything he is its slave as well; but our liberty-loving time thinks otherwise, and imagines that when one is not dependent on a ruler, then neither is one a slave, that when there is no ruler neither is there any slave. We are scarcely aware that it is servitude we are cultivating, and this is just what makes it so difficult to tear ourselves away from it. Because this bondage consists not in one man oppressing men (for then we should be aware of it) but in this, that men as individuals, forgetting their relation to God, in their relations among themselves become afraid of one another; that the individual becomes afraid of the group, whether few or many, in which also each man separately is moved by the fear of man, having forgotten God, and which holds together to form the Mass, relinquishing that patent of nobility that is given to each of us, the immortal honour that it is to be an individual.

About this, as indeed about so much else, a man may find himself put to the test in the world, may know the occasion when he must and ought to assert his conviction; but he will never be left without guidance if only he seek it in the right place—and where should that be, if not in Holy Scripture? Thus we read in the Acts of the Apostles that the apostles were forbidden by the Council to proclaim Christ. Nevertheless the apostles did not let themselves be terrified by this but they proclaimed Christ. Whereupon the Council had them apprehended, and would have had them slain, had not Gamaliel spoken against it. But the apostles were scourged, and thereupon were suffered to depart. Now where they were scourged we read in the Acts of the Apostles, vi. 41:[1]

And they departed from the presence of the council, rejoicing that they were counted worthy to suffer shame for his name.

With these words always before us we shall consider what everyone who suffers for a conviction may find to rejoice in, when he reflects:

THAT COURAGE IN SUFFERING CAN WREST THE POWER FROM THE WORLD, AND IS ABLE TO CHANGE DERISION TO HONOUR, RUIN TO VICTORY.

If we should suppose a youth well grounded in the truth, then we cannot in any degree refuse to admit that he knows what is true; and yet no doubt it will happen to him as it happened to others before him, that when he grows older he comes to know something very different, even though he still knows only what is true. The youth, to be sure, knows what

[1] This ought, of course, to be v. 41.

is true, but he has no knowledge of, he lacks experience of, the actual conditions, the total environment, within which the truth will be manifest. It is rare for a man from his earliest days to be helped towards this by shadowy apprehensions; far oftener than not the youth has the lovable trait of a confident simplicity, which sometimes may also be his handicap. The youth's eagerness for knowledge is such, and his willingness to appropriate to himself the truth as it is imparted to him, is such, that an inexperienced but beautiful imagination builds up for him a picture he calls the world, and on it what he has learned is set forth as on a stage. In the unspoiled imagination of the youth the one appears to be altogether suited to the other: the truth as he learned it in its purest form, and the world, the imaginary scene that he himself creates. Such, thinks the youth, must be the relation between the truth and the world, and so goes confidently forth into the world of reality.

But what does he discover there? Ah well, we shall not linger over all the defects, the mediocrity, the inconsistency, the pettiness, that he discovers, in the world that now surrounds him; we shall not pause at the sad discoveries the youth makes in relation to himself, how he himself also is not what he had supposed he was, how he comes to learn the truth of these words of Scripture, and maybe to read them sadly, "that he himself also is encompassed with infirmity":[1] we hasten on to a situation still more critical. For there are two ways in which the world may exhibit the opposite of what the unspoiled youth believed. Nothing of what he sees does this youth behold but with dismay, and even while he is uplifted by the divine glory of his own vision, still he shudders at the impression made on him by what he sees, which can prove to be uplifting only when seen with the eye of faith.

The youth has been instructed in what is true and what is good, taught to love what is good for the sake of the truth, and to flee the very appearance of evil. But now the world exhibits an inversion of this. There is an *inversion*, and we

---

[1] Heb. v. 2.

shall call it *impudence*; there are men who turn the scheme of things the other way round, and whose glorying, as the apostle says, "is in their shame",[1] while they "praise themselves for their infamy". Youth must behold it with horror; not only they do what is evil, but they do not even conceal it; not only they do not conceal it, but flagrantly do it; they seek out the light (though evil indeed is supposed to shun light); they lift up their eyes, and just by this are they known (though the guilty of conscience indeed is supposed to cast his eyes down); they not only do evil deeds flagrantly, but praise themselves for so doing, and "have pleasure in them that do them".[2]

But there is another way in which the world can show the reverse of what the unspoiled youth believed; there is another inversion which it is true holds in it the highest uplifting, although the sight is so terrible that the young man shudders because it finds no place in the beautiful conceptions of his imagination. And this is when the Good has to suffer in the world for the sake of the truth, when the world is seen to be unworthy of the good man, and the righteous man gets no reward, or rather is rewarded with scorn and persecution, when, finally, the confusion is so great that men think it pleasing to God to persecute such as witness to the truth, that is to say, when the good man is pressed to call shame honour, and, in a very different sense but with eternally valid truth, is pressed to transmute his own shame to honour. A youth can seldom indeed have thought of such a thing, he could but rarely have imagined it to be possible; it is usual, as it is most natural, for a youth to possess the winsome character of simple confidence, and that cannot understand such things as these.

When thus it happens, and preconceptions are shaken in a turning upside down more terrible than an earthquake, when truth is hated and its witnesses are persecuted—what then? Must the witness then go under before the world? Indeed he must. But is everything lost because of that? Nay, on the contrary. We hold this as a conviction, and find not the slightest

[1] Phil. iii. 19.   [2] Rom. i. 32.

need of proof, for if it were not so then such a one were not a witness to the truth. And therefore we feel certain that every such person must have kept to the very end a youthful memory, a memory of that which youth expected to find, and that he has had to examine himself before God, to discover in himself whether he might not be to blame. So that it still might be possible, so that it still might be, even as in youth he expected, what now for the world's sake he has wished for perhaps more than anything else, that in the world the truth should have its victory, and the good its reward. But when he is satisfied that it is not he who is to blame, and when he is satisfied that henceforward he must bear responsibility if he does not act, then courage rises up with more than human power, and he turns the relation the other way about and marvellously transforms the shame to honour, and takes it for his honour that he is therefore derided by the world, congratulates himself because of his persecution and his bonds and glorifies God that it is granted him thus to suffer.[1] *This inversion is the inversion of the courageous spirit*, and this too is the opposite of what an innocent youth had expected to see in the world. Woe unto him who with rashness, quick temper, and impetuosity would out of this horror of confusion bring a more peaceful situation! But woe unto him also who, when the need arose, lacked courage the second time to reverse all things reversed already once! Woe unto him! for if it is hard to endure the persecution of the world it is harder still to bear the eternal responsibility for having failed to act, to stand ashamed eternally because he did not achieve the courage to transform his shame to honour.

So did the apostles act, but it was WITH SUFFERING. Let us at once say here, what we must again and again repeat, that they did so with suffering; else would our discourse be substantially a daring lie, and if any were to follow it the consequence would be most terrible delusion.—After the apostles had been scourged they "departed rejoicing that they were counted worthy to suffer shame for his name".[2]

[1] cf. Phil. i. 12-30.   [2] Acts v. 41.

Many a terrible story there has been in the world of the delusions and the sins of men (we need but remember the ancient prophets and judges). But oh! the harshest of all reviling is not so terrible as is this apostolic courage. For even the harshest of reviling still admits of something in common, an affinity with those it punishes; that is just why it is so severe, it aims at their reformation; in passing sentence it condescends to deal with them. But in such a case as this, to come to the extreme that there is only one way left: to give God thanks and to rejoice that it is granted to one to suffer shame—this is, in comparison with even the harshest sentence, to speak with tongues. Can anybody, I ask you, think without shuddering of this situation; for if such a way of speaking is not very insanity, and so beyond all rule, then it is either the height of impudence or the miracle of courage. When one would describe the most corrupt and confused of times, could one, I ask you, describe them more truthfully, and yet more terribly as well, than by saying: the corruption and the confusion were such as to compel the good man to go to the limit of impudence, compel him to congratulate himself that he was put to shame!

But on the other hand if one wished to find the most adequate way of saying that the Good always prevails, how could one express it more adequately than by saying: That courage in suffering can wrest the world's power from it, and is able to turn shame into honour, victory into ruin!

For when we speak like this we are not saying that the good man some time in another world will be victorious, or that his cause some time in this world will be victorious; nay, but he conquers while he lives, in suffering he conquers while he lives, he conquers in the very day of suffering. When all human opposition is gathered together, yea, when a world rises up against him, he *is* the stronger; not even the restraining power of speech can hold him, he breaks through language, as it were, and by the help of God goes boldly forward, through everything, to compel honour out of shame, and victory from ruin. If it is with anxious misgiving that we watch the sleep-walker, walking no doubt with utter confidence over the abyss and yet also in a way we cannot comprehend: then it is no less with a shudder that we behold this apostolic confidence, which, at the very peak of insanity through God dares speak with tongues.

When Paul the apostle says: "With me it is a very small thing that I should be judged of you, or of man's judgment",[1] then these are certainly strong and weighty words, which we must not lightly repeat after him, for we do require to take account of human judgment also; but the language is still human. But this, this giving of thanks to God that one has been scourged, congratulating oneself that one has been held in scorn: this is what shocks us, for it is to count human judgment as less than small, as less than nothing. So greatly does it shock us, that avoiding delusions, whose aim is to evade danger, we venture to say from our hearts: Thank God we have not been tried like this nor brought to the point of making decisions involving such courage. For with the apostles there is no question of whimpering over trifles, no question of a few base, impudent men, such as at all times are to be found, even though there be many also with whom one longs to have in common, and does have in common, both language and thought. Nay, but the apostles stood alone confronting the world, nor was it only what we describe as the wicked part but the whole world that stood over against the apostles. And as to this relation to the world they had to make up their minds: That to be scourged was an honour, and to be held in derision an occasion for self-congratulation. In this way the apostles stood alone; for them there was but one thing, and as Paul adds, "all else is loss". Such words, alas, we repeat so often, and so often imitate, that at last we begin to think by perpetual repetition to fit them into our common everyday speech, from which they are worlds away; how many, I ask, are really capable of conceiving the courage that achieves such a victorious inversion

[1] 1 Cor. iv. 3.

as is implied in this language? When a man by his conduct shows himself but enthusiastic enough to be willing to make some sacrifice for a cause, even then he is almost regarded with sympathy as a simpleton, or deplored as deficient in mind. And yet there is no more in his enthusiasm than this, that he has such a love for a cause, as for its sake to be willing to bear the loss of something else, from among the good things of the world, as money, or reputation. But how far is not this still from the apostolic example! As for the enthusiastic man, he regards the possession of worldly goods as gain, though willing to give it up and bear the loss—the apostolic example considers possession itself as loss. Were anyone such an enthusiast as to reckon all worldly good to be nothing at all, why then, the world would come near to regarding him as a madman. And still such enthusiasm is less than apostolic, for the apostle not only reckons worldly goods as nothing at all, but regards them as loss. Just as a man, therefore, may have his own aspirations, after wealth, honour, and reputation, just so does an apostle aspire to flee from such good things; for in this all of us are in agreement, even the apostle, that all of us would fain avoid loss—only the disagreement is as great as it can be, for by loss we understand exactly the opposite of what the apostle understands.

Nevertheless, it is a cause for rejoicing with joy unspeakable that courage has this power to conquer, and is able, in spite of language and in spite of all the world, to put its impress upon thought, and that, let us not forget, with the veritable seal of godhead; so that what we whimpering simpletons call loss is to invincible courage gain, so that what the rebellious world calls shame is honour, and what the childish world names ruin is true victory; so that the language spoken by all a unanimous generation is inverted, and there is but one solitary mortal speaking human speech aright, he whom all the generation unanimously casts out.

But since the words of the Acts of the Apostles are our theme, and we ever have those words in mind in directing attention to the joyous truth that courage has through God such power, let us then try to understand the apostles, and how the apostles were conscious of themselves in this. For we ought indeed to confer about such words, and about the marvellous achievements of faith through courage. In spite of the calculating spirit that would hold us back, we ought to speak out, boldly and without reserve; for before God every man shall be eternally responsible who dares presumptuously to preach mere worldliness. We shall so speak, if we can, that everyone must shudder who in his presumption would dare to take such ways, and yet so speak that what affrights shall remind the rest of us how Christianity has had to struggle in the world; and then, if our lot is easier, in humble thankfulness we shall praise God, still duly honouring the apostles, honouring them with the frank and unreserved admission that it is a distinction before God to be granted so to suffer, yet with the frank and unreserved admission also that from such a distinction flesh and blood would rather be exempt.

For it is self-deception to make light of what distinguishes the apostle, as though it were, like wealth or talents, something that everybody would fain possess—and not to speak of it as the mystery of suffering, such that very nearly everybody would rather not be that kind of distinguished person, of whom it is required, as in fact it was required, that he should be, in thorough earnest, what an apostle was, "The offscouring of all things", "a spectacle unto the world".[1] And that is why we say, what the example of the apostles teaches, that it is the courage *that suffers* that is able to reach this wonderful height; the courage that acts cannot reach it. But then the apostles suffered all the time. Not only did they have sufferings, for he who acts can have sufferings too, but the whole course they followed was a suffering, their very bearing was submissiveness. They did not preach disaffection against the powers, but on the contrary recognised their authority, yet in suffering they obeyed God rather than men. They did not ask that they should

[1] 1 Cor. iv. 13 and iv. 9.

be exempt from any punishment, nor did they murmur when they suffered punishment, but when punished still continued to preach Christ. They would not compel any, but when themselves brought into subjection they overcame precisely by allowing themselves to be made subject. When the case stands otherwise, then courage cannot achieve the wonderful; for the wonder is just this, that what for all men seems to be their ruin, is for the apostles victory. If courage is less than this, it wants to act, it wants to be in the right itself, and to make men acknowledge the right; it neither will nor can in suffering endure the insane martyrdom of believing that what a world calls ruin, what a world labours under in the impression that it is ruin, that this in the mystery of faith through God is victory, that what a world calls shame, what a world labours under in the impression that it is shame, that this in the mystery of faith through God is honour.

"And they departed from the presence of the council, rejoicing that they were counted worthy to suffer shame for his name." This is the deepest conviction of the apostles, grounded in their hearts' trust in God; it is no affected saying, as when a man would hide the consuming heat of passion under a coldness of expression. Nay, for in no utterance of an apostle do we find enmity towards men; so greatly are they in friendship with God, conceiving themselves to be sacrificed, so uniquely obsessed with their relation to God, that thereby they have forgotten completely their relation to men. In truth they strive not with men; what men may do with them does not indeed concern them, or at most no more than as an occasion to seek in their souls their relation to God; in this alone, being quite absorbed in it, do they have their life.

Paul does not judge King Agrippa, in his speech he does not attack him, not by a word does he wound him, but on the contrary shields him, it is with gentle words and with reconciliation that he says: I would that not only thou, but also all that hear me this day were such as I am, except these bonds.[1]

[1] Acts xxvi. 29.

An apostle suffers, he strives not with men; and the reason is not that he wants to rise proudly superior above their assaults, oh, not that, but it is because he is occupied only with his own relation to God. This is at one and the same time the ever certain means of solace under suffering and the supreme exaltation. When all the world rallies all its powers against an apostle, it cannot succeed in striving with him on an equal footing, for the apostle has always that something more, which alone and altogether is for him his chief concern, which is everything for him: his relation to God.

Look now! to be put to death though innocent in any human sense, and to die with a witticism on one's lips,[1] that is a proud conquest, that is the triumph of paganism; it is moreover the supreme achievement in the relations of man and man; which is however to say, when God is excluded, and the whole of life and its greatest episode is indeed but a game, because God takes no part in it, for when he takes part then life is seriousness. An apostle, on the other hand, excludes all else, forgets all else, he does not see it, does not hear it, is not aware of it, he has but God in view; and that is how we hear from the martyr the humble words: "I thank God it is granted me to be counted worthy to be crucified." Words such as these are not spoken to make mockery of men; nay, for the humble martyr, men simply are not present, he has nothing to do with them, their evil and their ignorance claim no part of his attention, he does not demand that he shall carry the day against them, nor want to show that he is truly the stronger: nay, but he turns to God, even in his last moment, not without fear and trembling lest he has not really accomplished his task, but also with trust and with devotion, giving humble thanks that he has been esteemed to be worthy of a shameful death.

Look now! a raging mob crowds round the martyr; it imagines that the issue is between him and them, even at his last moment jeers at him, and then waits to hear either complaining cries

---

[1] Socrates; *v.* Plato's *Phaedo* 118A.

or else disdainful words from him who suffers. It is hidden from the eyes of the mob that Another is present, yet so it is, and the martyr sees only God, and only to God does he speak. His words indeed sound as if they were spoken in mockery of the deluded mob, but they are not spoken so, for the martyr is speaking to God, and is giving thanks that he has been counted worthy of this suffering. And the words perform wonders; he does not come down from the cross, but he does something yet more wonderful, by courage reversing the meaning of words. When the most fervent language would hardly suffice to describe the innocence of this martyr, and by the same measure, humanly speaking, his due reward, he feels, just because he is not dealing with men but is in the presence of God, that he merits no reward whatever, he tears in pieces his reckoning with men, he bequeaths to them all their wrongdoing, and humbly gives thanks to God; as we others give thanks for whatever is good, so he gives thanks for the favour of being crucified. What a wonderful way to speak, what a wonderful exaltation, as if at the very height of insanity, to have such a courage! For consider, my hearer, I beg thee, what it means to give thanks to God for the favour of being crucified! We, what do we do, we, who whimper and complain when the world goes somewhat against us, we, so anxious to be in the right, who are proud to be in the right, we, who, did we speak truth, would confess that we come near to calling that way of speaking insanity!

"They departed rejoicing", when they had been scourged. They really did rejoice. It was not an appearance assumed as long as the world was looking on. They did not affect it in order to show the world how they despised it. Nay, but they really did rejoice, and never maiden was more joyful on the day of her betrothal than were the apostles on that day of their scourging and on every such a day that for them was a day of plighting their troth with God. He who dedicates himself to a cause, and sets out to *win*, is glad indeed for the victory of his cause, not for the victory's sake alone, but because for him the victory is an assurance he is going by the way by which he meant to go, for what has happened now is what he expected to happen. But he who dedicates himself to a cause, and sets out to *fight*, is glad in the day of persecution, for what has happened now is what he was bound to expect, and accords with his whole outlook. In the first instance victory is no fortuitous price of good fortune but of the very nature of the case; and in the second instance this is the reason for rejoicing, that suffering comes not as a fortuitous piece of bad fortune, but in the very nature of the case. If victory had not been realised for the first of these two men then no doubt he would have sought the fault as being in himself; if persecution had been lacking for the second, then no doubt he would have sought the fault as being in himself. This is very easy for every man to understand who has any idea what it means to have a view of life and to live by it, and who does not, on the contrary, live by the mere chance of a throw of the dice.

And what now of an apostle? He had seen the crucifixion of the Holy One, he had seen all the evil and corruption of the world made manifest, when his Lord and Master was held in derision: with this stamped on his mind he went forth into the world. Try then and see if thou canst imagine otherwise than that this man must desire to have the same world treat him the same way, that this man must with a desperate and deep anxiety accuse himself if he were not persecuted, apprehensive only about this one thing, that it might be too great an honour to be crucified! Try it. Imagine that he who was to proclaim to the world the message of a Holy One crucified as a malefactor between two thieves, that he himself should be robed in the splendour of purple, that he should have all the good things of the world for his possession, this man who was to proclaim the teaching of One who had been crucified, how that his kingdom was not of this world. Try it; if indeed thou canst bear to try it, and if it does not refuse to be tried, because the mere thought of such a thing is like presumptuous mockery of the apostle! And so it is just as it should be, and the apostles with all sincerity before God rejoiced that they had been scourged.

Or else imagine that the proclaiming of Christianity by the apostles had quickly triumphed, as it is said to have done, and that an apostle might have had some experience of the danger by which later generations were tried, so that power and glory and might were offered them, not to refrain from preaching Christ, but to preach him: would an apostle, let me ask, have been quite pleased to persuade himself that he understood it, or would it not have been more than he could understand, that his Lord and Master should be treated as a criminal, and the disciple who is "not above his master" should achieve honour and dignity? I ask, in short, whether an apostle would ever so have changed that, in his outlook on life and Christianity, instead of avowing himself a fighter he would have avowed himself a conqueror? For the outlook of the conqueror assumes that the great majority, the mass of mankind, are on the average adherents of truth, and for that very reason it is one's distinction and excellence that are marked by having power and honour. But the outlook of the fighter teaches him that the Good must suffer reverses, and for that reason its servants are persecuted, derided, treated as malefactors and fools, yea, and just by that are they to be recognised, yea, and just for that reason they will not have power and honour, for if they did it would imply a falsehood concerning their outlook. Only he may freely take to himself honour and power who holds the conviction that the race is on the average good, and that may indeed be sometimes true, so that on the other hand it may be the distinguishing mark of a morbidly distorted enthusiasm that one will not accept honour and power when one deserves to have it.

The apostles rejoiced that they had been scourged, and they rejoiced in sincerity. Perhaps too they had thought of the words: Every sacrifice shall be salted.[1] It may be that to one danger the apostles were less exposed, inasmuch as in those

[1] Mark ix. 49.

times it was every day and every moment a matter of a life and death struggle. Let us look at this danger so that we may the better understand the joy of the apostles in being mocked and persecuted. In more peaceful conditions, when everything seems so secure, when men say: Peace, peace! when the temporal seems to have a charmed existence, then is the danger only too imminent that a man himself should be inclined, and that other men should help him, to receive the Spirit in vain. Then they would proffer what they call admiration to him who is gifted, would admire his special excellence, and would like to forget that it is all the gift of God, and would help the favoured one to forget it too. Then they accept honour from one another, play the game of "surprises", and whether admired or admiring waste their life like fools, so misusing it as to make existence savourless because it lacks salt, or like a sweetmeat because it has no seriousness. Imagine an apostle to have come upon anything like this, imagine him who surely was endowed more highly than ever was mortal man, and yet who always humbly understood that before God he was as nothing, to have discovered that men would take in vain the gift of grace entrusted to him, and would help him do the same, would deck him out in purple and in frippery, and let God be forgotten: would he not, I ask, in holy wrath have torn such harlot-bonds to shreds, would he not, I ask, have thought of the joy he knew when existence was not hollow, when it had a savour, when an apostle went away rejoicing after being scourged, and truly did rejoice in it?

We have now considered what is joyous in the reflection that courage has such a power to conquer. We have also recalled how the apostles are found to have their place in such a thought. We dare not keep back from anybody the joy, the triumphant joy, that thought contains; we dare not hide the truth that courage has this power. But neither have we made it a careless remark, a casual utterance; but, on the contrary, as far as possible, to the joy we have added the weight of every serious consideration, in order that we might if we could discourage hastiness. For this joyous thought is not like a so-called harmless remedy that can be used on any and every occasion without danger, and is used for a slight cold; but it is like a drastic remedy, the use of which is not without danger, but which, rightly used, is in truth salvation from a sickness unto death. No doubt it will seldom happen in our day that a man may dare to say with truth he suffers for Christ's sake, and we would again and again urge a composing of the mind, to reflect that one cannot make the same plea as was appropriate for the relation of the apostles to a pagan world. Yet even if this be exceptional, it may nevertheless happen frequently, and it may happen with any man—if indeed he does not wish "to draw back into perdition"[1]—that he may come to suffer for a conviction. But in this contention for a conviction we are not fit to strive without the support of courage. According to the greatness of the danger, so there is given, we hope and believe, the courage from above, and even in dangers not so great there is still a need of courage. And so, whoever thou art, if thou hast that which thou callest thy conviction (and sad indeed it were didst thou have none), and if it is required of thee to fight for it: then seek thou not the world's support and the support of men. For such support is treacherous enough, sometimes to such a point (and even this is not the real point of danger) that it disappoints and fails us in the hour of greatest difficulty, but sometimes also (and this is the true danger) to such a point that when it is given freely it stifles the good cause. For even as many a cause, it may be, has been lost because the support of the world was lacking, so too has many a cause been ruined because the world was allowed to help. Nay, but seek courage with God. If perchance thou dost suffer for a conviction, or art preparing to suffer for a conviction, or with all seriousness art thinking of what can happen to a man: then for a moment do thou rejoice for the joyous truth that was the subject of our discourse. But err thou not; rest not pleasantly in this joyous truth; rather strive earnestly to

[1] Heb. x. 39.

find courage with God; then will the joyousness come to thee in yet fuller measure. A conviction is not anything one must hasten to publish to the world: abundant confusion and grievous injury has, alas, been wrought, because one who was immature has published his immature conviction. Nay, let but the conviction grow in silence, let it but grow along with the courage gained with God, and then shalt thou, in whatsoever danger may assail thee, be certainly assured what courage can do. A spark in wood-shavings is extinguished with a glass of water, but when it has had time bit by bit to take hold of all the house, and at length utters a deep groan (what happens in our illustration happens actually in the spirit's experience which it illustrates), and it bursts out in flame—then say the firemen: Here there is nothing to be done, the fire has conquered here! Grievous is it indeed when the firemen say: Here there is nothing to be done; but joyous is it when the fire that has conquered is the fire of conviction, and they that are hostile say: Here there is nothing to be done! For if the fire of conviction has had time bit by bit to take hold of a man, until, when the moment has come, with a deep groan it releases the blast of courage into the flames: then in suffering courage is capable—and this too can be called a thrilling sight, when burning zeal for a conviction consumes a man like fire!—is capable of wresting power from the world, and is able to transform shame into honour, ruin into victory.

Then let us every one hold fast this precious truth, this joyous thought of courage, so that nobody may take our courage from us. For even though we may freely acknowledge our conflict in the world to be but trivial and of small significance in comparison with that of those glorious ones who were tried in the greatest of all issues, yet would it be of no small significance should we in our insignificant conflict lose our courage.